DUSTBOWL DESPERADOES

Gangsters of the Dirty '30s

STONE WALLACE

FOLK
LORE
PUBLISHING

The Publisher: Folklore Publishing
Website: www.folklorepublishing.com

National Library of Canada Cataloguing in Publication

Wallace, Stone, 1957–
Dustbowl desperadoes: gangsters of the dirty '30s / Stone Wallace.

(Legends series)
Includes bibliographical references.
ISBN 1-894864-10-7

1. Gangsters—United States—Biography. 2. Outlaws—United States—Biography. 3. Crime—United States—History—20th century. I. Title. II. Series: Legends series (Edmonton, Alta.)

HV6785.W34 2004   364.1'092'273   C2004-901349-1

Project Director: Faye Boer
Cover Image: Courtesy of The Library of Congress

Photography credits: Every effort has been made to accurately credit the sources of photographs. Any errors or omissions should be directed to the publisher for changes in future editions. *Photographs courtesy of* Kansas City Public Library (title page; p. 239); Library of Congress (p. 16, USZ62-112142; p. 30, USZ62-92411; p. 46; p. 79; p. 92; p.95, USZ62-125405; p. 103, USZ62-125405; p. 107; p. 118; p. 127; p. 142; p. 163; p. 178; p. 180; p. 185; p. 196; p. 204; p. 207; p. 225); National Archives, Still Pictures Branch (p. 29, 306-NT-677-41; p. 52, 65-AN-26; p. 68, 306-NT-9443; p. 230, 65-AN-17; p. 242, 65-AN-16); Randy Stephanson (p. 165).

We acknowledge the support of the Alberta Foundation for the Arts for our publishing program.

PC: P5

The Alberta Foundation for the Arts

Alberta COMMUNITY DEVELOPMENT

COMMITTED TO THE DEVELOPMENT OF CULTURE AND THE ARTS

Dedication
To Cindy, the best moll a make-believe tough guy
could ask for

ACKNOWLEDGMENTS

BEFORE WE JOURNEY back to an era of dirt-road dastards, Thompson submachine guns and getaway Ford flivvers, permit me a moment to thank a few people whose various generous gifts have made the writing of this book both a pleasant and rewarding experience.

First and foremost, I would like to acknowledge the encouragement and support provided by my publisher, Folklore Publishing, destined to become one of the leading historical publishing houses in Canada. I most especially want to thank Faye Boer, the publisher every author hopes to find, whose expert and ongoing support proved invaluable in the writing of these pages. Beyond our professional association, I am even more pleased to consider Faye a cherished friend.

Many thanks to Randy Stephanson, who supplied the photo of Clyde and Buck Barrow's gravesite.

I would also like to thank Kelsey Kowalchuk for providing reference material; Corey Graham and Shannon Roy for technical support; and Paulina Spakowski, Curtis (who, when interest in the concept of this book was first expressed, moved me into action by saying "Now all you have to do is write it.") and Lauren Urbanowich for their moral support through the writing of this and other projects.

And thank you to Cindy, who always believed in me, even when I had trouble believing in myself.

Contents

Introduction

"He ain't a gangster; he's a real old-time desperado.
Gangsters is foreigners. He's an American."

–"Gramps" Maple describing killer-at-large Duke Mantee,
The Petrified Forest, 1935

LIKE THE DUST-WHIPPED WINDS that ripped across the drought-laden landscape of the American Southwest, the gangsters and gunmen of the 1930s hit fast and hard, with a fury that, although soon extinguished, left in its wake death, destruction and bitter memories.

They enjoyed a brief moment of infamy, but theirs was not a life to be envied. It was more of an "existence" that saw them forever on the run, trusting no one, with no rest and little sleep and awakening each day to the realization of kill or be killed.

They were the product of their time—that bleak moment in history known as the "Dirty 30s"—a swirling period of transition, coming off the heels of a decadent yet carefree era where wealth, prosperity and boundless optimism permeated much of the country.

As the Jazz Age trumpeted to a close with the repeal of Prohibition in 1933, the nation was already suffering under the Great Depression following the economic collapse of "Black Tuesday," October 24, 1929. Virtually overnight, the gaiety ceased as princes became paupers, and families became destitute.

Suddenly, the American Dream had become a mockery. The value of the country's money declined by 38 percent. Twelve million unemployed men, dazed and confused, rode the rails seeking any sign of work. Others sold apples on street corners or stood in soup lines.

In rural America, bank failures and foreclosures forced more than 38 percent of farmers off their land. But the worst was yet to come as the economic drought was soon eclipsed by a drought of natural origin that would blanket much of the southwestern prairies with devastating results.

As the country plunged deeper into despair, President Herbert Hoover's assertion that "Prosperity is just around the corner" had a hollow ring for most Americans. For many, the repeal of Prohibition was strangely anticlimactic. For others, it ushered in a new age of lawlessness.

Prohibition: the 18th Amendment to the Constitution of the United States that became law at 12:01 AM on January 17, 1920. The country's Noble Experiment had far-reaching consequences that, in retrospect, one needn't have been clairvoyant to predict. The so-called "dry years" gave rise to a new breed of entrepreneur—capitalists in the truest sense of the word. Most of these men presented an outward veneer of respectability, conducting their business affairs in professional settings. But just a thorn scratch beneath the lining of their expensive pinstriped suits lurked a corruption and ruthless ambition that would leave bloodstains on the historical tapestry of America. Such was their perverse influence on society that almost 80 years later we still recognize their surnames—Capone, Luciano, Lansky, Siegel.

Each of these men grew up hard and learned early to fight for what was theirs. As they reached adulthood, they continued to fight, only now to retain and expand city territories.

The makeshift weapons of their youth—bricks, clubs and brass knuckles—took on a new and deadly efficiency as gangs became proficient in the use of explosives, pistols and, of course, the famed "trench sweeper" of World War I—the Thompson submachine gun. Chicago, Detroit and New York became violent playgrounds for the racketeers and beer barons in whom the erosion of human morals was steadily perpetuated by the enormous wealth they accumulated through crime and corruption. At the height of his power, for example, Al Capone's annual income was estimated to be $30 million!

But as greed and the grab for power bred more violence, culminating in the St. Valentine's Day Massacre of 1929, public indignation reached a fever pitch, and previously apathetic politicians were forced to take an aggressive stance against the country's criminal menace.

"Scarface" Al Capone became the major target. His criminal empire was enormous, including bootlegging, gambling, prostitution and labor racketeering. His attempts to elicit public sympathy by establishing soup kitchens throughout Chicago during the early days of the Depression were met with contempt rather than gratitude. The writing was on the wall, as blunt as the bloodstained bullet holes at 2122 North Clark Street. The Big Guy's reign was over.

While Capone detested most of the sobriquets applied to him, he was rather flattered to be called (if only by intimates) "Snorky," an underworld slang term meaning "elegant." In many ways it was his openly extravagant lifestyle that proved his downfall. The treasury department had serious concerns regarding Snorky's income—especially since he had somehow neglected to file a tax return for 10 years.

Capone couldn't muscle or buy his way out of that rap, and he was handed the harshest sentence the judge could impose. The "celebrity gangster" was hustled aboard a train to Leavenworth and later transferred to Alcatraz. After his release, Capone returned to his mansion in Florida where he died in near anonymity, a position that he would have been wise to observe in life.

Unlike the flamboyant Capone, the new mob kingpins, such as Anthony Accardo from Chicago and New York's Meyer Lansky, chose to maintain low profiles. They were wise enough to know that if their various illegal enterprises were to survive, let alone prosper, they would have to operate as faceless entities. They also knew that they would have to become organized. Arbitrary grudge killings must cease. The rackets would now be run by committee. The slate was made clean by the assassination of the Old World "Mustache Petes" in what became known as the "Night of the Sicilian Vespers." On the night of September 10, 1931, 40 members of La Cosa Nostra around the country were murdered by gunfire to allow for the emergence of the new order of the Syndicate.*

Yet hardly had the smoke cleared from the gun battles of the 1920s when a new breed of misanthrope stepped into the existing socioeconomic climate. These were not the pseudo-business types possessed of the boardroom brilliance of Capone, Accardo or Luciano. Most were the ill-educated sons (and daughters) of farmers and hillbillies. Unlike their big-city counterparts, these criminals had not honed their skills through youthful (yet profitable) extortion and protection rackets. Rather, they embarked on their lawless pursuits with reckless abandon, taking their cue from the outlaws of the Old West.

With the Depression at its height, these back-road bandits, driven by hunger and desperation, set out on robbery and kidnapping sprees that saw them emerge from the plains of

---

*Some historians maintain the assassinations never took place, and that the Night of the Sicilian Vespers is part of Mafia folklore. In any event, no one has ever been able to assemble a list of the supposed victims.

Indiana, the dust bowl of Oklahoma, the hills of the Ozarks and the open fields of Texas. They moved swiftly and hit without mercy. In 1933, the country recorded 12,000 murders, 50,000 robberies and 3000 kidnappings.

While their careers were (mercifully) short, their earnings paltry compared to the millions that poured into the coffers of big-city crime bosses and their grimy lifestyles hardly infused with the Hollywood glamour of a Bugsy Siegel, these Depression-era lawbreakers continue to captivate the imagination because of the sheer audacity of their exploits. They truly were modern-day cowboys, although advanced in the tools of their trade. Thompson submachine guns capable of dispensing 550 slugs a minute replaced the Winchester rifle. And instead of hopping onto a horse to make their getaways, these outlaws leaped onto the running boards of fast-moving Fords. (Clyde Barrow was so impressed with the performance of Ford vehicles during high-speed chases that he personally wrote a letter to the company president praising their product. Needless to say, his comments were not used in their advertising.)

They were Dustbowl Desperadoes, and their names and crimes have made them legends.

John Dillinger—America's first and most famous Public Enemy. He was the era's most wanted criminal, yet it was never proven that he'd ever actually killed anyone. His many exploits have become legendary, including his celebrated break from "escape-proof" Crown Point Jail. And while the "official" version states that federal agents shot John Dillinger dead in Chicago, facts have since come to light suggesting that Dillinger may not have been the man killed outside the Biograph Theater.

Baby Face Nelson—the era's most terrifying bank robber and gunman. Lester Gillis, aka George Nelson, although slight of build and possessed of an innocent, almost child-like face, carved himself a reputation so ferocious that he was not only feared by the public, but shunned by the underworld as well. He killed for the sheer joy of killing, and when he finally shot it out with federal officers, he refused to die until he first brought down the two agents who had cornered him.

Pretty Boy Floyd—the most incongruously named outlaw, Charles Arthur Floyd was neither pretty nor very boyish. He was a fearless bank robber and murderer, yet a devoted husband and father, who is still remembered by many hill folk as a benevolent benefactor. His most notorious claim to infamy was when he was named as one of the gunmen in the 1933 Kansas City Massacre, an accusation that he would always deny.

Ma Barker—long thought to be the criminal mastermind behind the Barker-Karpis Gang. Although she died alongside her youngest son in a hail of bullets after a lengthy FBI siege, many claim that Kate Barker was really just a harmless hillbilly whose posthumous notoriety stems from the FBI's attempts to justify why they had shot to death an innocent old woman.

Alvin "Old Creepy" Karpis—the last of the era's big-time public enemies who, ironically, hailed from Montreal, Canada. A confessed bank robber and kidnapper, Karpis, like Dillinger, may never have committed a killing during his lengthy career. He was the only criminal ever to be personally captured by J. Edgar Hoover (a claim that Karpis denied), and he spent more than 25 years in Alcatraz, longer than any other inmate in the prison's history.

Bonnie Parker and Clyde Barrow—a pair of aberrant psychopaths whose murderous exploits throughout the Southwest earned their gang the label "The Bloody Barrows," far removed from the romantic couple portrayed onscreen by Warren Beatty and Faye Dunaway. They managed to shoot their way out of several police traps until a posse led by former Texas Ranger Frank Hamer decided to play as fair as they did.

George "Machine Gun" Kelly—the most hyped and overrated of the '30s bad men. George Kelly was a second-rate bank robber and kidnapper who was dominated and controlled by his wife. Kelly believed his own publicity and enjoyed flaunting his tough guy image, yet his capture, although perpetuated in myth, remains the most anticlimactic of the era.

Francis "Two Gun" Crowley—the model for some classic gangster film characterizations. The teenage Francis Crowley was a city-bred celebrity wannabe, a small-time thief and psychopathic killer who, prior to his capture, shot it out with more than 300 New York police officers in what was called "The Siege of W. 90th Street."

Roger "The Terrible" Touhy—Chicago bootlegger and Capone associate in the 1920s. Touhy became a second-rate underworld figure during the '30s, whose primary claim to infamy was his spectacular break from Statesville Prison in Joliet, Illinois, where he was serving time on a phony kidnapping rap (masterminded, most likely, by remnants of the Capone mob). Still, he'd made some powerful enemies during his career, some of whom eagerly awaited the old gangster's release from jail.

The Kansas City Massacre—perhaps the most brazen act of violence ever committed by the underworld. Intended as a plot to free Oklahoma bandit Frank "Jelly" Nash, the escape attempt went horribly wrong (or "according to plan"), resulting in a bloodbath that cost the lives of four lawmen and their prisoner, Frank Nash. Although a prime suspect in the massacre, Pretty Boy Floyd maintained his innocence to his dying day.

Violent lives. Violent ends. In some instances even for the heroic enforcers of law and justice who pursued and, on occasion, were pursued by these bandits and murderers. Yet through their criminal exploits, the Dustbowl Desperadoes were instrumental in changing laws and helping to advance previously outdated methods of crime detection. The following pages reintroduce the reader to the gangsters and public enemies of yesteryear. These biographies are flavored with little-known facts and anecdotes gleaned from many years of research, and more importantly, a lifetime of interest. Many facts presented in this book will no doubt surprise you. Given "official" records and personal conclusions, they may even shock you.

Above all, I hope you are entertained by this look back at an era that stands as a midway point between the taming of the frontier and today's world of sophisticated technology. The era and its people, for better or for worse, left an indelible mark on the fabric of America during a vulnerable period in the nation's history—and whether for sociological or historical purposes, their contribution should not be forgotten.

CHAPTER ONE

John Dillinger
(1903–19??)

"I guess my only bad habit is robbing banks."

–John Dillinger

ONE CAN ONLY IMAGINE those final thoughts that coursed through the brain of Public Enemy Number One John Dillinger as consciousness slowly ebbed from his body. Certainly, even as each breath grew increasingly harder to pull, the gangster couldn't accept that he was dying. He'd escaped too many bullet-riddled ambushes and police chases to acknowledge a death so inconsistent with his derring-do image.

Yet as the deepening shadows closed in around him, John Dillinger's eyelids fluttered shut as one final suffocating breath lodged in his throat. The man FBI chief J. Edgar Hoover wanted more than any other as his department's prize catch was dead.

John Dillinger died, not in the heat of a gun battle on the cold pavement of a city street, but on a cot in the back room of a weather-beaten two-story shack on Chicago's north side. He succumbed not to a fatal bullet, but to an accidental overdose of ether administered by a nervous medical assistant during preparation for a plastic surgery procedure.

The date was May 28, 1934, less than two months before history recorded John Dillinger's "official" death outside the Biograph Theater in Chicago.

John Dillinger is recognized as the archetypal Depression Day Desperado, and his gang is credited with pulling off some of the most spectacular bank robberies of the era. But Dillinger, though quick, athletic and daring, was also a calm, careful and methodical man who always played the percentages before embarking on a job. He was also often the voice of reason among the murderous upstarts in his outfit. While he could be as threatening with an automatic or tommy gun as any other outlaw of the time, Dillinger only resorted to gunplay when cornered, and even then, never with the intent to kill.

Had Dillinger been taken alive and stood trial, it is interesting to speculate on his fate. Most likely, he would have been sentenced to death. But more so for his reputation than his crimes. Both the press and law enforcement agencies took delight in labeling John Dillinger everything from an "arch killer" to (in Hoover's words) "a super-rodent who used women as a shield."

In truth, Dillinger was neither. He was simply a bank robber—a bandit possessed of a certain charisma who could charm female tellers even as he held them at gunpoint. He was not a cold kidnapper like Alvin Karpis or a psychopathic murderer such as Clyde Barrow (although members of Dillinger's outfit certainly had no qualms about living up to the latter distinction). Yet, because of his high profile and his being tagged Public Enemy Number One, Dillinger was portrayed as the nation's most ruthless criminal, every law-abiding citizen's worst nightmare.

Admittedly no candidate for Boy Scout leadership, the real John Dillinger had a pleasant, easygoing nature. When compelled

John Herbert Dillinger, the most colorful and charismatic outlaw of the era, who patterned his own criminal exploits after his boyhood hero, Jesse James

to use force, as he often was, he fired only to wound or disarm. The story goes that the only killing of which Dillinger could even be remotely accused occurred during a robbery, when he shot a pursuing patrolman in the leg. As the man fell, he dropped into the line of gunfire between fleeing gang members and the police and was killed. Whether apocryphal or fact, the incident gives a fair portrayal of John Dillinger's character.

People who knew Dillinger recall a man completely unlike the (in)famous image. Alvin Karpis remembered Dillinger as a "quiet guy with a gentle manner and speech" who enjoyed reading dime-store western novels. And the many ladies in his life told of a soft-spoken, courteous gentleman with an infectious grin. When pressed, even some lawmen whose paths crossed Dillinger's later admitted to having a grudging respect for the outlaw.

While the law might have jeered Dillinger, the public mostly cheered him. In 1934 during a newsreel showing of the gangster, a Justice Department official in attendance reported to his superiors that the audience erupted into applause when Dillinger's image flashed on the screen. Although the public may have been momentarily chilled by biased news reports detailing John Dillinger's latest criminal exploit, they were even more thrilled by his bank robbing derring-do at a time when many were seeking even a temporary escape from the poverty and monotony of their lives.

The story of John Dillinger has taken on legendary proportions throughout decades of media hyperbole, further perpetuated by countless books and movies that focus on the sensational and mostly fictionalized elements of his life and crimes. Yet such exaggeration is hardly necessary. The true story of John Dillinger is even more compelling than the myth.

Dillinger's reign as the nation's most wanted criminal lasted a mere 12 months, between June 1933 and July 1934, but during that time he and his gang robbed more banks and stole more money (reportedly over $500,000 in Depression dollars) than Jesse James did during his 16 years as an outlaw. When Dillinger was finally (supposedly) brought down, it had to be achieved through the combined effort of five states and the FBI.

Not too shabby for an Indiana farm boy.

John Herbert Dillinger (the original pronunciation emphasized a hard "g") was born June 22, 1903, in Indianapolis, Indiana. His mother, Mollie, was a frail woman who died following an apoplectic seizure and failed operation when John was four years old. His father, John Wilson Dillinger, who was of hard-working stock, ran a grocery store and owned several houses. These activities left him with little time to spend with his son. Johnny's upbringing was left mostly to his older sister, Audrey. The two were close, and while John, Sr.'s work ethic and Germanic stoicism often made him a cold and distant figure to young John, it was Audrey who assumed the role of the indulgent parent. She married shortly after her brother's birth, and even though she mothered seven children of her own, she claimed to have "adopted" Johnny as her own child.

When John Dillinger, Sr. remarried in 1912, his paternal attempts grew even more awkward. Audrey continued to be young John's primary caregiver, especially after their stepmother gave birth to half-siblings Hubert in 1914 and Doris in 1916. Audrey actually admitted that she was closer to Johnny than to her own children.

Despite a less-than-traditional home life, Johnny was a bright student who achieved above-average grades at Washington Elementary School. He was popular with his classmates and a talented athlete, excelling at baseball.

But John possessed a wild side that at times pushed him to extreme behavior. One such episode brought him before a magistrate. Charged with stealing coal from the Pennsylvania Railroad yards and selling it to neighbors, the 12-year-old John appeared in court with a defiant attitude. He stood before the judge, assuming a cocky stance and chewing a wad of gum. When the magistrate ordered the boy to remove the gum from his mouth, John obeyed by sticking the gum to the bill of the cap on his head.

The judge was not amused. "Your mind is crippled," he admonished the boy.

Johnny merely grinned.

He was turned over to the custody of his parents, and his father decided that a change of atmosphere might curb the boy's wild streak. He sold his store and houses and purchased a modest farm in Mooresville, 17 miles south of Indianapolis.

Unfortunately, the old man's hope for a more productive life for his son had exactly the opposite effect. John dropped out of high school and even refused to help his father with farm chores. He took a job as an apprentice machinist at the Reliance Specialty Company, where his supervisor praised his manual dexterity and gave equally high approval for his work conduct. But John was restless. To please his stepmother, he made another try at school, but classroom study and discipline continued to bore him, and he dropped out for good during his first semester at Mooresville High.

John, Sr.'s efforts to interest his son in farming also met with ongoing resistance.

"I liked the land, but John never did," the old man said years later. "Said it was too slow. I guess the city got ahold of him."

And indeed it had. When not working, John drove to nearby Martinsville, where he and his friends would drink beer and shoot pool.

While school and his machinist's job held no appeal for the teenage Dillinger, he still retained his passion for baseball. Some of his restless energy was more positively channeled when he joined the Martinsville baseball team. He proved to be an exemplary second baseman.

When John began seriously dating his Uncle Everett's step-daughter, Frances Thornton, it seemed as though the boy might steer himself back on track. But when John asked his uncle for Frances' hand in marriage, Everett vehemently refused.

"There's a boy from Greencastle who's had a fancy for Frances," Uncle Everett explained. "Comes from a prosperous family. Sorry, Johnny, but can't no way give my blessings to a boy like yerself with no prospects." (In 1933, Dillinger would pull off his biggest heist at the Central National Bank in Greencastle!)

John was stunned. He also felt betrayed, not only by his uncle, but also by his sweetheart. Embittered, he returned to Indianapolis, where he embarked on a drinking and whoring binge that cost him his job and left him with a severe case of gonorrhea. Finally, on the night of July 21, 1923, John further vented his frustration by impulsively stealing a car.

Abandoning the car and fearing arrest, John, again acting on impulse, enlisted in the United States Navy. But he had no more enthusiasm for a career at sea than he'd displayed for school or legitimate employment. He went AWOL several times and finally jumped ship for good on December 4, 1923, when his ship docked in Boston. (Dillinger's battleship the USS *Utah* would be destroyed exactly 18 years and 3 days later during the attack on Pearl Harbor). The Navy listed Dillinger as a deserter, and for the first time a reward of $50 was posted for his capture.

John Dillinger returned home where he again found romance, this time with 16-year-old Beryl Ethel Hoving. After a brief courtship, he married the starry-eyed girl in the spring of 1924.

Dillinger possessed an enormous sex drive, but he remained a restless soul with little interest in other marital responsibilities. The couple argued loudly and often about Dillinger's frequent late-night drinking and pool-playing excursions.

On the evening of September 6, 1924, after another bout of bickering with Beryl, Dillinger had several beers with Edward Singleton, an ex-convict who was also the Martinsville team's umpire. Singleton saw a way to make some quick money, and he asked Dillinger to join him.

"That grocer, Frank Morgan, carries the week's receipts home late on Saturday night," Singleton explained to the intoxicated but interested youth. "All we gotta do is meet him along the way."

Later that night, the two men jumped the grocer as he made his way home along the quiet street. Although he was hit over the head and roughed up pretty good, Frank Morgan managed to wrestle away a pistol carried by one of the attackers. A shot went off, startling Dillinger and Singleton, who ran off into a side alley without the money.

The local deputy sheriff suspected that Johnny Dillinger was one of the would-be thieves and, together with a forehead-bandaged Morgan, went out to the farm to question him. Morgan, who knew the Dillinger family, at first refused to believe that John was in any way involved. But Dillinger was persuaded by his father to admit the truth, and in the end, he tearfully confessed.

Dillinger was promised leniency by the prosecutor if he pleaded guilty. However, he had the misfortune to appear before Judge Joseph W. Williams, a man of severe reputation who promptly handed down two concurrent sentences of 2 to 14 years and 10 to 20 years on the two charges of felony and assault with intent to rob. The judge also fined Dillinger $100 on each charge and disenfranchised him for a period of 12 years.

(His cohort in crime, Edward Singleton, got a more lenient sentence, although he ultimately received harsher justice when years later he fell into a drunken sleep on a railroad track and was decapitated by a train.)

Dillinger's punishment was unusually stiff. Deputy Sheriff Russell Peterson, who delivered Dillinger to prison, later commented: "John was just a kid. He got a raw deal. You just can't take 10 years away from a kid's life."

At the age of 21, John Dillinger began his stay in the Indiana State Reformatory at Pendleton. Perhaps as a survival technique, Dillinger employed the same cocky attitude he had as a kid to establish his own ground rules.

"I won't cause you any trouble except to escape," he told Warden A.F. Miles.

Miles was unimpressed. "I've heard that before."

Dillinger just smirked. True to his word, on the night of October 10, he made his first break for freedom. It was an admirable effort, although a thorough search of the prison grounds soon led to his recapture a few hours later.

Undeterred, Dillinger tried escaping three more times, and while none met with success (instead he got an additional year and a half tacked on to his sentence), his audacious reputation brought him to the attention of Homer Van Meter and "Handsome" Harry Pierpont, who were both seasoned criminals and incorrigible prisoners at Pendleton.

The pair befriended Dillinger and took him under their tutelage, even though the two disliked each other personally. Unfortunately, when the walls of Pendleton could no longer control the disruptive behavior of Van Meter and Pierpont, they were transferred to the Indiana State Prison at Michigan City. Dillinger missed his pals. But circumstances dictated that he would soon rejoin them. During his brief time at Pendleton, Dillinger's unimpressive conduct had not gone unnoticed, nor had his skills as a baseball player.

At his parole hearing in 1929, he was told by the board chairman: "It is the finding of this board that you have not yet recognized the debt you owe society. Therefore, it is our unanimous recommendation that you be denied parole at this time."

Again, Dillinger was hit with a hard judgment. He was stunned by the verdict, but he figured that if he had to stay in prison, he might as well be with Pierpont and Van Meter. He requested a transfer to serve out his sentence at Michigan City, explaining with a grin: "They have a real ball team up there."

Governor Harry G. Leslie granted Dillinger's transfer, and on July 15, he was shipped to his new "home."

Dillinger's graduate course in crime really began at Michigan City. Through Pierpont and Van Meter, he was introduced to such hardcore bank robbers as John "Three-Fingered Jack" Hamilton, Charles "Fat Charley" Makley, Russell Clark and a former Prussian soldier and associate of the notorious Baron Lamm, Walter Dietrich. They were patient teachers, and Dillinger was an eager student.

By this time, Dillinger had thoroughly committed himself to pursuing a life of crime. When he was finally paroled on May 22, 1933, he exited the prison gates as a hardened, embittered ex-con, determined to take back from society in monetary gains what they had taken from him in years.

Dillinger was in every way a free man; his wife had divorced him in 1929. Throughout the summer of 1933, John Dillinger put into practical use the lessons he had learned at Michigan City and embarked on a robbery spree in order to raise funds to finance a jailbreak for Pierpont and the others. Forced to recruit second-rate "talent," Dillinger was also often frustrated when he came upon a bank closed by the Depression.

"How's an honest bank robber supposed to make money in these times?" he lamented.

Still, he managed to pull off some impressive scores, establishing his athletic, charismatic image by vaulting over high railings into tellers' cages. And while Dillinger took his business seriously, he always treated accommodating bank employees with polite respect.

"He was the most courteous bank robber," remembered cashier Margaret Good. "I think he knew I was a kid, and he didn't want to scare me any worse than he had to."

Dillinger soon met and fell for Evelyn "Billie" Frechette, a member of the Menonomie Indian tribe in Wisconsin. Although

Dillinger had—and would have—many girlfriends, the raven-haired Billie Frechette remained his most faithful love.

Dillinger needed one more lucrative score before he could facilitate his friends' escape from Michigan City. On September 6, he pulled off Indiana's second-biggest robbery when he hit The State Bank of Massachusetts Avenue, Indianapolis, for $24,800. On that occasion, he again displayed the athletic agility that had become his trademark when he hurtled himself onto a seven-foot barrier and, while jauntily seated atop the bar, announced to the startled assistant manager: "Mister, this is a stickup."

With his bankroll, Dillinger purchased several guns and bought a fast car. Then on the night of September 12, he drove to Michigan City, where he crept up to the athletic field and tossed the paper-wrapped guns over the 30-foot-high fence. The plan was for Pierpont and the others to go to the field the next morning before work detail and retrieve the guns. However, another convict got to the package first and turned in its contents to the deputy warden.

Dillinger purchased new weapons and traveled to Chicago, where he bribed a foreman to open a barrel of thread destined for the prison shirt shop. He carefully placed the guns inside the barrel, which was then resealed and marked with a red "X" as prearranged with Pierpont.

Dillinger decided to take a rest and visited another girlfriend, Mary Longnaker, who lived in a boardinghouse in Dayton, Ohio. He barely had time to remove his hat before two detectives brandishing shotguns burst into the room.

Dillinger merely raised his hands in the air and said, "Nice to see you."

Just four days later, Harry Pierpont stood before nine convicts who had chosen to participate in the Michigan City break and announced, "Okay, boys, if you're ready to take the chance, we go now."

The group, armed with the firepower Dillinger had smuggled in to them, forced two guards to escort them to the front gates. Without even a single shot fired, the convicts calmly walked out of the administrative building entrance and drove off in two cars that were parked in front.

Through Dillinger's efforts, 10 convicts made the greatest mass prison escape in Indiana history. Their liberator, however, was sitting in a Lima, Ohio, jail cell awaiting arraignment for a bank job he'd pulled in Bluffton or the arrival of his pals, whichever came first.

Pierpont and the others had not forgotten Johnny and were in the process of reciprocating the favor he'd done for them by putting together "traveling funds" to the tune of $25,000 from two successful holdups.

On the evening of October 12, at precisely 6:20 PM, Pierpont, Makley and Clark walked into the Lima jail and approached Sheriff Jess Sarber. The sheriff had just finished a hearty dinner of pork chops and mashed potatoes and was relaxing with his wife and his deputy, Wilbur Sharp.

"What can I do for you fellas?" Sarber asked pleasantly.

Pierpont did the talking. "We're officers from Michigan City. We want to see the prisoner, John Dillinger."

"I'll have to see your credentials," Sarber told them.

Pierpont squinted. "Here's our credentials," he said as he withdrew his pistol and fired twice into the big man's gut.

Sarber's deputy was also quickly overpowered and ordered to hand over the keys to Dillinger's cell. Makley saw Sarber try to lift himself from the floor. He darted over and smashed the butt of his gun against the sheriff's head. Once free, Dillinger walked into the outer office where he saw Mrs. Sarber cradling her dying husband.

While Dillinger had no love of the law, he'd been treated well by Sarber, and he said to Pierpont, "Did you have to do this?"

Pierpont, as merciless as he was handsome, responded with a blank stare.

From the moment the "Terror Gang" (as the criminals were initially dubbed by the press) exited the Lima jail, they spent their remaining days on the run from the law. They headed for Indianapolis, where Dillinger again took up with Billie Frechette, and they made plans to procure weapons for a series of bank robberies.

Their next stop was Peru, Indiana, where the gang raided a police arsenal and collected enough handguns, machine guns, shotguns, rifles and ammunition to supply a small army.

Throughout the fall and winter of 1933–34 and into the spring, the gang embarked on a bank-robbing spree the likes of which the Midwest had never seen. On October 23, they pulled off their first job at the Central National Bank in Greencastle, Indiana, which netted the outlaws their biggest haul of $75,346. During the heist, Dillinger approached a stack of bills on the cash counter next to a trembling farmer.

"That your money or the bank's?" Dillinger asked him.

"Mine," the farmer replied.

"Okay, keep it," Dillinger said. "We only want the bank's."

Unlike other desperadoes of the era, Dillinger and his men were meticulous in planning their robberies. They had learned a great deal from their Michigan City mentor, Walter Dietrich, who had instructed the gang to approach each job with military-like precision and strategy. Following Dietrich's lessons ultimately resulted in 11 successful bank heists for the gang.

The key men of the outfit were Harry Pierpont, the most daring and fearless of the group; John Hamilton, the most experienced; and, of course, John Dillinger, whose natural criminal attributes soon had him assuming leadership of the gang.

Actually, it was Captain Matt Leach of the Indiana State Police who began calling the outfit the "Dillinger Gang." He'd tried it out as a psychological ploy to create dissention among the outlaws, claiming that it was really Dillinger and not Harry Pierpont who was the true mastermind behind the gang. What Leach hadn't counted on was the lack of competitive ego between the two, and that Pierpont was happy to let Johnny get the credit for their successes.

But the gangsters were beginning to receive negative press. On January 15, 1934, in East Chicago, Indiana, Patrolman Patrick J. O'Malley tried to intercept the bandits during a $20,000 bank heist and was machine-gunned to death, reportedly by John Dillinger. But he always maintained his innocence, not only in killing the police officer, but also in the robbery itself.

Such publicity troubled Dillinger. Although he'd always had a fascination with firearms and could handle a pistol or tommy gun with marksman-like skill, he proudly considered himself "the slowest gun in the Midwest" when it came to displaying this talent in his profession. He avoided violence wherever possible and frequently criticized the quick-draw antics of contemporaries Pretty Boy Floyd and, most particularly, Clyde Barrow.

Although at least 15 murders would eventually be leveled against the gang, usually occurring during wild police shootouts, authorities were hard-pressed to conclusively attribute even a single killing to Dillinger. When fleeing a police trap, he would often fire his machine gun, but only into the air, to create a diversion. And if cornered into using force, he was more inclined to club a man unconscious with the butt of his gun than shoot him.

Regardless, the violent reputation of the Dillinger Gang continued to grow, as did statewide police dragnets. Dillinger managed to elude heavily manned roadblocks in both St. Paul and Chicago, but each escape was becoming narrower. Thinking a change of climate might be in order, Dillinger, Pierpont, Makley and Clark sped off in separate cars to rendezvous in Tucson, Arizona.

The move proved to be a bad one. A fire in the hotel where Charles Makley and Russell Clark were rooming brought them into contact with firefighters who recognized their faces in a copy of *Police Gazette* magazine the following day.

The firemen contacted the Arizona police, who moved swiftly. On the morning of January 25, 1934, Clark was pistol-whipped while resisting arrest. Later that same day, Charles Makley was apprehended while browsing in a local store. Then Harry Pierpont was picked up "on suspicion." When asked to accompany police downtown to answer a few questions, the volatile gangster drew a pistol from his belt, which he promptly dropped when the cold barrel of a shotgun was pressed against the side of his head.

As Harry Pierpont eyed each of his captors, he spoke with typical belligerent bravado. "I'll remember you, and you and you! I can break out of any jail. I'll be back, and I won't be forgetting."

Finally, police staked out the house where Dillinger had been staying and arrested him. As he sat in police headquarters, he retained his calm composure and talked amiably with the arresting officers.

The arraignment, which was held the next morning at the downtown justice court building, attracted a crowd estimated at 2000. Already telegrams and phone calls were coming in from Indiana, Ohio, Wisconsin and Illinois, each state demanding the right to try the outlaws.

It was finally decided that Dillinger would be extradited by plane to Indiana to stand trial for the East Chicago killing of Patrolman O'Malley. Pierpont, Makley and Clark would be taken by train to Ohio, where they would face charges for the murder of Sheriff Sarber.

On January 30, Dillinger was met with celebrity-like excitement when his plane landed at Chicago's Municipal Airport. A 13-car escort drove the outlaw to Indiana and took him directly

The "Terror Gang" awaits arraignment in a Tucson courthouse following their capture in Arizona. "Handsome" Harry Pierpont sits at Dillinger's right.

to the Crown Point Jail. Termed "escape proof," the heavily fortified facility was patrolled around-the-clock by armed deputies as well as by vigilantes brandishing rifles and shotguns who wanted to discourage any attempt to free Dillinger.

All the while, Dillinger carried on as if he didn't have a care in the world. He posed jauntily for photographs alongside Sheriff Lillian Holley (whom he confessed to "likin' just fine") and prosecuting attorney Robert Estill. Estill, who had political aspirations based on his successful prosecution of the gangster, drew damning criticism when a picture was published showing him responding to Dillinger's elbow-resting-on-the-shoulder gesture by draping his arm around the sardonically smiling outlaw.

Dillinger knew that he would have to plan and execute his own escape from Crown Point. Legend has it that he carved a crude-looking pistol from a washboard, blackened it with shoe polish and then thrust it at the jailer who was making his rounds. Dillinger then systematically disarmed the other guards on duty and locked them inside his cell.

The story of the wooden gun has become central to the Dillinger myth and has been retold and recreated numerous times in book and movie biographies of the outlaw. But that may not have been the way it happened.

A wooden gun was made, but Dillinger may not have crafted it. Many crime historians claim that the gangster had made arrangements through his lawyer Louis Piquett to bribe a guard to pass him a real gun. Once Dillinger made his break, officials were so embarrassed by the ease with which Dillinger and fellow prisoner Herbert Youngblood breached their "escape-proof" jail (not to mention effecting their getaway in Sheriff Holley's own car) that the wooden gun was hastily prepared to present to the press to cover up the bribe and sidestep the resulting negative publicity.

However, Dillinger himself lent credence to the wooden gun story when shortly after his breakout he wrote to his sister Audrey saying: "I am sending Emmett (Audrey's husband) my wooden gun, and I want him to always keep it. I see that Deputy Blunk says I had a real .45. That's just a lot of hooey to cover up because they don't like to admit that I locked up eight deputies and a dozen trusties with my wooden gun before I got my hands on the two machine guns, and you should have seen their faces."

According to a hostage, Dillinger's jailbreak had him jubilantly singing *Get Along Little Dogies* as the sheriff's car rolled along Ohio side roads. However, his escape also brought him into the jurisdiction of the FBI when he violated the Dyer Act against interstate auto theft by crossing the Illinois State line.

While federal agents had been tracking Dillinger for some months at the request of various police agencies, the FBI could now intensify their search for the elusive outlaw. FBI Director J. Edgar Hoover used the Bureau's vast resources to track down and apprehend the nation's number one criminal, devoting countless hours to the outlaw's capture. Agents underwent specialized training for an anti-crime force, practicing marksmanship on targets that bore the smirking likeness of John Dillinger.

Meanwhile, Dillinger drove to St. Paul, where he began to assemble a new gang. He hooked up with old friend Homer Van Meter, who brought in Eddie Green and top wheelman Tommy Carroll. To Dillinger's added delight, he re-teamed with John Hamilton. But the gang needed one more member, and on Van Meter's (reluctant) recommendation, they recruited former Chicago bootlegger and small-time racketeer Lester Gillis (aka Baby Face Nelson).

Impressed despite himself to be part of Dillinger's mob, Baby Face Nelson, all 5'4" of him, wanted to make it clear that he would be running the show. Van Meter, fiercely loyal to Dillinger, would never allow such an arrangement and argued violently with Nelson, leaving it to the diplomatic Dillinger to smooth the tension. Dillinger explained to the more reasonable Van Meter that it was more important to free Pierpont, Makley and Clark, whose fates were almost certainly sealed for the murder of Sheriff Jess Sarber.

But no matter what Nelson might have believed and regardless of how the other gang members might placate his ego by

J. Edgar Hoover (1895–1972), FBI chief and the subject of both personal and professional controversy throughout his lengthy government career

~⋘✕⋙~

acknowledging his crazy plans, no one doubted that John Dillinger was in charge. Nelson's approach to bank robbing was manic. He wanted the bandits to rush inside and start shooting.

On March 6, 1934, the gang hit the Security National and Bank Company in Sioux Falls, South Dakota. The robbery went smoothly until the cop-hating Nelson spotted an off-duty police officer getting out of his car. Suddenly, leaping onto a desk, Nelson cursed as he fired his machine gun through the plate glass window.

Ecstatic that he'd downed the officer, Nelson began whooping, "I got one of 'em! I got one of 'em!"

Shocked by the outburst, Dillinger and the others were forced to rush the robbery before more cops arrived on the scene. They still managed to drive off with $49,000.

Eddie Green was assigned to case out the gang's next job, and on March 13, 1934, Dillinger and his companions marched into the First National Bank in Mason City, Iowa. Almost immediately, things went wrong. Gunfire erupted, resulting in bullet injuries to both Dillinger and John Hamilton. The gang took 20 hostages in their escape to discourage reckless police pursuit.

While Dillinger recuperated from his shoulder wound in a St. Paul rooming house with his girlfriend Billie Frechette, he wrote upbeat letters to his sister Audrey, then brooded over the fate of Harry Pierpont and Charles Makley. As he had expected, both were sentenced to die for the Sarber killing. Russell Clark received a life sentence because of the jury's recommendation of mercy. Dillinger was powerless to help any of them.

Dillinger did, however, enjoy a laugh at Pierpont's reported remark to the prosecuting attorney: "I'm not a man like you, robbing widows and orphans. You'd probably be like me if you had the nerve."

Pierpont may have had the last word, spoken with his customary arrogance, but time was running out for the killer. Taking his cue from Dillinger's much-publicized Crown Point escape, in September 1934, Pierpont and Makley carved pistols from cakes of soap in a desperate attempt to escape death row. Their efforts resulted in Makley being fatally shot by guards and Pierpont seriously wounded. One month later, "Handsome" Harry

Pierpont was strapped into the electric chair at the Ohio State Penitentiary in Columbus, and his soul was sent into eternity.

Dillinger's angst was compounded by frequent reports naming him the most wanted man in America. He had the title of Public Enemy Number One: Wanted Dead or Alive, and clearly, there really wasn't a preference about how he was brought in.

On the night of March 31, 1934, federal agents tracked Dillinger to the Lincoln Court Apartments. Billie Frechette stalled them while she alerted Dillinger, who grabbed a machine gun. Homer Van Meter happened to be coming up the stairs, and he drew on the agents before making a getaway. As the agents gave chase, Dillinger burst into the hallway, spraying machine-gun fire as he and Billie escaped down a back stairway. One of the agents fired a shot as they raced into the alley, catching Dillinger in the leg. The pair managed to reach their car, and with Billie behind the wheel, they sped off in reverse down the alley and squealed out onto the street.

Once again Dillinger was lucky. While having his wound treated, he realized it was too close a call. Only the unexpected intervention of Homer Van Meter had saved him. He decided to leave St. Paul for a while. A fringe member of the gang suggested a fishing retreat on Spider Lake in northern Wisconsin.

"And this piece of paradise is called...?" Dillinger asked.

"Little Bohemia Lodge."

Dillinger liked the idea, but he and Billie first paid a visit to the Dillinger farm in Mooresville. Although the authorities were anticipating such a move and watching the property, the outlaw managed to slip by, enjoying a day with family and friends. At one point, his father took him aside and gently suggested that he surrender himself to the law. Dillinger shook his head ruefully and said that it was now too late. He doubted they'd even give him the chance to give himself up alive.

Shortly thereafter, Dillinger and Van Meter raided the police arsenal in Warsaw, Indiana, to replenish their weapons and ammunition. The two then drove separately out to Little Bohemia Lodge to join the other gang members.

Meanwhile, J. Edgar Hoover had assigned the task of apprehending Dillinger to Melvin Purvis, head of the FBI office in Chicago. Although young and hardly a physically intimidating presence, Purvis (who was fastidious to the point of changing his shirt three times a day) had already proven himself as one of the Bureau's most reliable agents.

Purvis was eager. Hoover said to him, "Get me Dillinger, and the world is yours." But the former lawyer also knew that bringing in the gangster alive might prove to be a hollow victory. Dillinger's only federal offense was when he had driven the stolen car across a state line following his break from Crown Point. And while he was still facing a murder indictment for the slaying of East Chicago Patrolman Patrick O'Malley, his lawyer had produced a witness who swore that Dillinger was in Florida at the time.

What most frustrated Purvis was that public sentiment was for Dillinger. People crushed by the Depression were actually rooting for the bad guy. Many were either vicariously escaping the deprivation of their own lives through Dillinger's exploits or they believed that the law was unfairly hounding him.

When Purvis got the tip that John Dillinger and members of his gang, including Homer Van Meter and Baby Face Nelson, were enjoying a vacation in Wisconsin, the G-man* assembled his squad and prepared to move on the lodge.

---

*Although the term "G-men" was long attributed to Machine Gun Kelly during the gangster's cowardly capture, the name, which reputedly translates into "Government Men," was more likely the result of an FBI public relations campaign during its formative years when the Bureau was seeking public endorsement and support. The reference "G-Men" became so popular that it was used as the title of a popular 1935 James Cagney film.

After months on the run, Dillinger found solace in the secluded wooded slopes of Spider Lake. A popular summer resort town, Spider Lake had little patronage during the early part of the year, and Dillinger felt that he could relax without fear of being recognized.

Unfortunately, he was. On the night of Sunday, April 22, 1934, all hell broke loose at Little Bohemia Lodge. As Purvis and his men crept up on the lodge, dogs started barking, alerting Dillinger and the others. Moments later, three shadowy figures whom Purvis assumed were gangsters walked out the front door. They had been drinking and failed to heed Purvis' warning to halt. Purvis gave the order to fire, and all three went down, one fatally wounded.

Grabbing their weapons, Dillinger and his gang, with the exception of Baby Face Nelson, who was with his wife in one of the cottages, followed their planned escape route through a second-story lakeside window. Dillinger, Van Meter, Tommy Carroll and John Hamilton raced along the shore and into the woods. Meanwhile, Purvis and his men fired rounds into the main floor, believing that the gangsters were trapped inside.

Suddenly, Baby Face Nelson burst out of his cottage. Firing two automatics, he traded shots with Purvis while backpedaling into the woods. His attempt to steal an automobile owned by a nearby resort owner was thwarted when a car containing two federal officers and a police constable arrived on the scene.

Instead of fleeing, Nelson ran right up to the car and began firing his automatic, killing Special Agent W. Carter Baum instantly and wounding the other two men. Nelson shoved the bodies from the car and squealed off into the night.

And when the FBI agents entered the lodge the following morning, all they found were the gangsters' terrified girlfriends huddled in the basement.

The fiasco at Little Bohemia severely tarnished the image of the FBI. Not only had all the gangsters escaped, but a federal agent had also been killed. In addition, the FBI had gunned down three innocent men who were later identified as John Hoffman, a gas station operator; John Morris, a cook; and Eugene Boiseneau, a specialist (the latter two were from the nearby civilian corps camp). Hoover was harshly criticized for the bungled raid, and a petition began to circulate demanding Melvin Purvis' suspension from the Bureau. Hoover responded immediately by posting a $10,000 reward for Dillinger's capture. The reward was in addition to the $10,000 already offered by the five states where Dillinger had robbed banks. But it would take a lot to soothe the ire of a nation.

Humorist Will Rogers wrote: "Well, they had Dillinger surrounded and was all ready to shoot him when he come out, but another bunch of folks come out ahead, so they just shoot them instead. Dillinger is going to accidentally get with some innocent bystanders some time, then he will get shot."

On leaving the resort, Dillinger, Van Meter and John Hamilton drove a stolen car back to St. Paul. Just 20 miles from their destination, their car attracted the suspicion of three county policemen who took off in pursuit. Dillinger was an excellent driver, and while he skillfully negotiated the unfamiliar road, Van Meter and Hamilton leveled machine-gun spray out the back windows.

The police pulled their pistols and returned fire, hitting Hamilton square in the back. Although Dillinger managed to elude their pursuers, the car was riddled with bullets and began sputtering. The gangsters were forced to abandon it and hijack another vehicle.

Dillinger decided to drive into Chicago, where he could both cool his heels with members of the Barker-Karpis gang and perhaps find an underworld doctor who could patch up Hamilton. Because of the severity of Hamilton's wounds, the outlaws had to drive slowly, so it took them three days to reach

Chicago. By that time, Hamilton was beyond help. Gangrene had set in, sending a raging infection throughout his body. All Dillinger and Van Meter could do was quietly sit by and wait for their friend to die.

After Hamilton expired, Dillinger and Van Meter took the body to a nearby quarry where they dug a shallow grave and poured lye over Hamilton's face and hands to prevent his identification.

"Sorry to do this, Red," Dillinger said, solemnly, "but I know you'd do the same to me."

Dillinger didn't have long to mourn. He was hotter than ever. Although the FBI suffered most of the blame for Little Bohemia, Dillinger got his share of bad press (given that he was the target of the assault), resulting in a waning of public support. With his face prominent in newspapers, newsreels and on wanted posters throughout most of the country, Dillinger decided to undergo plastic surgery. His lawyer, Louis Piquett, referred him to a German-born specialist who had served time on a narcotics charge and was in desperate need of cash.

Dillinger was dubious. "But is he good?" he wanted to know. "Some of these makeup artists are so unsteady I wouldn't trust 'em to carve a turkey."

"Dr. Loeser's a magician with a scalpel," Louis Piquett assured him.

Dillinger handed over the $5000 fee and told his lawyer to make the necessary arrangements. The operation took place on May 28, 1934, at a rundown building owned by a former speakeasy operator. Dillinger arrived under cover of night and was told to expect Dr. Loeser the next morning.

Dillinger felt comfortable with Dr. Loeser, but less so with his young assistant, whose nervousness was apparent. He explained the work he wanted done, including the removal of his fingerprints. He then lay down on a cot while Dr. Loeser went to wash his hands, and his assistant began administering ether through a towel mask.

But the assistant quickly realized that he had given Dillinger too much ether too soon when the gangster began turning blue. He had swallowed his tongue and had stopped breathing. The assistant frantically called for Dr. Loeser, who rushed into the room and used forceps to pull Dillinger's tongue from his throat.

It was too late. Dillinger's heart had stopped beating. Dr. Loeser immediately began artificial respiration. It took Loeser several attempts, but finally Dillinger began breathing again on his own. Dr. Loeser went on to complete the surgery once Dillinger was stable, but the results were far beneath Dillinger's expectations.

After his surgical ordeal, Dillinger decided to lay low. However, on May 30, just two days after his surgery, he was alleged to have robbed the Merchants National Bank of South Bend, Indiana, for $18,000. He then returned to Chicago.

Dillinger was alone and lonely because Billie Frechette had been taken into custody right before Little Bohemia and was now serving a two-year jail sentence. He began seeing a 26-year-old waitress named Polly Hamilton, whom he'd met in a Chicago restaurant. Polly's co-workers, although charmed by her new boyfriend, began teasing her by saying that he "looked a lot like Dillinger."

Polly was a recent divorcee, and she roomed with an older woman who called herself Anna Sage. Her real name was Anna Cumpanas, and she was facing deportation for operating a brothel. She was desperately seeking a way to stay in America. So when she discovered the real identity of Polly's new beau, she quickly contacted an old acquaintance, Sergeant Martin Zarkovich of the East Chicago Police Department, with a proposition.

She told Zarkovich that she knew where John Dillinger was and would help set him up for capture if she was paid the reward money and got her deportation order stayed.

Apparently, Zarkovich first went to Chicago Police Captain John Stege with Sage's information, adding that he would reveal her proposal only if Dillinger was killed, not captured. Stege bluntly refused the cold-blooded proposition, so Zarkovich went directly to Melvin Purvis. Purvis approved the plan and later met with Anna Sage. While he told her that he could offer no guarantees regarding her deportation, he promised to do what he could for her.

Purvis relayed the information to J. Edgar Hoover in Washington, whose instructions were succinct: "Get Dillinger at all costs."

Sunday, July 22, 1934, was swelteringly hot. Downtown Chicago registered temperatures in excess of 101°F. Anna Sage told Purvis that Dillinger would be taking both her and Polly to a movie in an air-conditioned theater that night, but they hadn't decided which picture to see. They'd narrowed their choices to the Marbro or the Biograph.

Purvis stationed agents at both theaters. He personally staked out the Biograph, where he watched for a woman wearing a bright orange dress. It wasn't difficult for Purvis to spot the "Lady in Red" (which was the color her dress appeared under the marquee lights) as two women and a man entered the theater shortly before the 8:00 PM feature.

Melvin Purvis later admitted that he could not truthfully identify the man accompanying the two women. He recalled that the man was dressed casually in a light-colored shirt and was wearing wire-rimmed sunglasses and a straw boater. Still, Agent Purvis knew that he was looking at his quarry. The plan was to get Dillinger as he exited the theater. The wait began.

The FBI hadn't notified the local police of the stakeout, and when the theater manager grew suspicious of the men loitering across the street, he summoned the police. Purvis and his men promptly ushered them out of the way.

The movie that Dillinger and his companions had chosen was *Manhattan Melodrama*, a gangster picture starring Clark Gable. It ended at approximately 10:30 PM with its famous final scene of Gable cheerfully walking the last mile to the electric chair. The theater patrons walked from the air-conditioned coolness of the theater into the still-stifling night air. Purvis' hands trembled as he prepared to light a match to his cigar. This was his signal to his fellow agents that Dillinger had left the theater. Then, his squinty eyes focused on the red hue of Anna's dress. Anna and Polly flanked the young man as the three walked arm-in-arm by Purvis.

After two unsuccessful tries, Purvis finally lit his cigar, and the agents moved in.

"Stick 'em up, Johnny!" Purvis was reputed to have ordered.

The man broke free of his companions and dashed towards an alley. It is said that he reached into his pocket for his gun, a Colt automatic. But before he could draw the weapon, agents opened fire. The man pitched face forward onto the pavement.

Only two shots actually penetrated their target. One lodged in the victim's left side; the other was a 100-to-one shot that entered his stooped back and exited out his right eye.

Pandemonium ensued. Upon hearing that it was John Dillinger who had been shot, crowds converged on the scene, many hoping to obtain macabre souvenirs—handkerchiefs, paper and even torn pieces of clothing were dipped into the dead man's blood.

The carnival atmosphere continued at the Cook County morgue where the body was transported. After the corpse was washed, photographers and the public were allowed inside. Lines outside the morgue stretched for more than a quarter mile, with people coming back two or even three times for a viewing.

A macabre scene was played out in the aftermath of the killing. A barker passed through the crowd outside the morgue selling watches stained with the dead man's blood. Even the police were not exempt from such ghoulish behavior—one Chicago officer actually shook the corpse's hand. But most macabre of all was that the slain man's brain mysteriously disappeared following the autopsy.

In the aftermath of the shooting, Melvin Purvis rushed to call J. Edgar Hoover, who was elated by the news. A little boy at the scene, however, displayed another emotion.

With tears streaming down his face, the boy tugged at a spectator and asked, "Is it true, mister. Did they really kill John Dillinger?"

To this day, the truth behind John Dillinger's death remains in question. While all "official" reports are quite clear that it was indeed John Herbert Dillinger who was killed outside the Biograph Theater, there are those who, upon closer examination of the evidence, have come to the conclusion that the slain man was not Dillinger, but a small-time hoodlum named James Lawrence.

To support their theory, they have presented several arguments. Firstly, Dillinger was intelligent. He'd eluded the law on numerous occasions thanks to his smarts and razor-sharp intuition. Since Little Bohemia, he'd kept himself out of the spotlight (except for one suspected bank score), realizing that he'd lost public sympathy and that he was fair game for anyone looking to collect the $20,000 reward. It therefore seems inconceivable that a man taking such careful precautions would risk exposing himself in a crowded movie theater.

Secondly, Dillinger never really trusted women, even Billie Frechette, about whom he once warned gang members: "She's an Indian. Never give her a drink." If Dillinger could express these doubts regarding the one woman who remained consistently loyal to him, he surely would have been wary of Anna

Sage, an immigrant whorehouse proprietor whom Dillinger must have suspected had her own opportunistic agenda.

Also, it is necessary to take into account Dillinger's character. He was not a mad-dog killer like Baby Face Nelson, ready and eager to shoot it out with the cops. Rather, he was a man who preferred to avoid gunplay. It simply was not in his nature to recklessly draw on federal agents he could never hope to outgun.

Finally, the compelling postmortem evidence displayed physical inconsistencies between the dead man and John Dillinger. Morgue photographs show a face only remotely resembling Dillinger's famous visage, the more prominent discrepancies not attributable to the plastic surgery Dillinger had undergone. Dillinger's eyes were blue; the dead man's were brown. The corpse was shorter and heavier than Dillinger's recorded height and weight. The body possessed scars (including one from abdominal surgery that Dillinger had never undergone), wounds and birthmarks which Dillinger's records fail to report. And there was evidence that the dead man had a congenital rheumatic heart condition, which certainly would have precluded Dillinger's famed athletic abilities. Such evidence points to the conclusion that John Dillinger had escaped his own execution.

The theory is that the gangster suspected a trap and that he either persuaded James Lawrence to take his place that fateful night or that Lawrence volunteered to prove to Dillinger that his suspicions of being lured into a trap were unfounded. A third consideration is that Lawrence was deliberately set up as the fall guy in a scheme of intricate intrigue.

And why was Martin Zarkovich, a man with strong underworld ties, so insistent that Dillinger not be taken alive? Was he actually part of a conspiracy that was arranged with heavy cash payments from Dillinger's lawyer Louis Piquett to ensure the gangster's escape? He could not allow Dillinger to be taken alive because it would not be Dillinger who would be arrested.

If this theory is correct, then Anna Sage's role in subsequent events must be investigated. Perhaps she, like so many other women, was charmed by the charismatic gangster. And while she could not bring herself to betray Dillinger, she still had her own interests to consider. It is logical that through her association with Martin Zarkovich, a compensation package was arranged through Louis Piquett (from Dillinger's substantial bankroll). With her cooperation, the package would be further enhanced by FBI reward money (authorized by Melvin Purvis). She was guaranteed that her participation would be limited to fingering a lookalike decoy.

Although there may never be a definite solution to the puzzle, it is known that Anna Sage received only $5000 of the posted reward money and that her request to remain in America was denied. In 1938, the infamous "Lady in Red" was sent back to her native Romania. Reputedly, it was J. Edgar Hoover himself who used his considerable influence to block Sage's stay of deportation.

Theories abound, but John Dillinger's "death" remains one of history's truly unsolved mysteries. Except, of course, by John Dillinger himself. With the heat finally off, it is easy to imagine this Depression Day good/bad guy making his final escape into a life of peaceful (law-abiding?) anonymity.

CHAPTER TWO

The Roundup

"Today, I'm the only man who knows the 'who's and how's,' and as my end comes very shortly, I'll take this little story with me."

–"Handsome" Harry Pierpont, moments before his execution

WITH JOHN DILLINGER OUT OF THE PUBLIC SPOTLIGHT, either as a result of federal bullets outside the Biograph Theater in Chicago, or more likely, a wisely chosen retirement following the much-publicized event, the FBI had rejuvenated its image in the eyes of both the public and the press.

Quickly capitalizing on national headlines proclaiming its efficiency against gangsterism in America, the Bureau under J. Edgar Hoover's stern and watchful direction sent its agents into high gear to clean up the remaining "vermin." And the remnants of the Dillinger Gang were naturally at the top of Hoover's extermination list.

Of the nation's 10 most wanted criminals, seven belonged to the Dillinger Gang. Of the original members, John Hamilton was dead, as was Charles Makley, both killed by police gunfire. "Handsome" Harry Pierpont, although almost crippled during the same prison shootout that had ended the life of his friend Makley, kept his date with "Old Sparky." Russell Clark survived these turbulent years locked behind bars, and

Melvin Purvis (right) delivers his "official" report on the Dillinger slaying to boss J. Edgar Hoover (left) and U.S. Department of Justice William Stanley (center).

when finally paroled in 1970, he died of cancer just a few months later.

Although not officially a member of the Dillinger team, murderer Herbert Youngblood shared the distinction of accompanying the gangster in his celebrated escape from Crown Point. On parting company with Dillinger following the breakout, Youngblood seemed to disappear off the face of the earth. Rumors began to surface that maybe Dillinger had killed the black man to silence him. But cold-blooded murder wasn't Dillinger's style.

Youngblood finally turned up in Port Huron, Michigan, where on the night of Wednesday, March 14, 1934, he made the rounds of colored saloons in the city, flashing his bankroll and bragging about his association with the famous John Dillinger. Youngblood continued his obnoxious behavior into Friday morning, when police were summoned to a small store to deal with an intoxicated customer.

Three lawmen tried to subdue Youngblood, who suddenly drew his pistol and fired on them, killing Undersheriff Charles Cavanaugh, critically wounding Deputy Howard Lohr and hitting Sheriff William Van Antwerp in the arm. A customer, who was also shot by Youngblood, managed to retrieve the gun of one of the lawmen from the floor and fired two rounds into Youngblood. Van Antwerp and Lohr also discharged their weapons, and Youngblood fell, mortally wounded, with seven slugs in his body.

Eddie Green was the first of the Dillinger Gang to go. His was the only death to precede the shootout at Little Bohemia. Green had helped get Dillinger to a doctor after the police raid at the Lincoln Park Apartments in St. Paul. Dr. May, the physician tending to the gangster's superficial wound, suggested that Dillinger recuperate in Eddie Green's apartment, but Green threw up his hands.

"Not a chance," said Green. "It's too hot."

But Green agreed to drive Dillinger to a sort of clinic operated by a nurse known to the doctor. It was a hush-hush setup whose main clientele were women seeking abortions and those suffering from venereal disease. It was an illegal operation, but no one would think to look for Dillinger there. Dillinger recovered quickly, and just days later, he must have considered himself lucky that he had not been taken to Eddie Green's apartment. Eddie hadn't even had time to clear out his belongings before federal agents raided the building. They soon discovered that Green had arranged with two maids to collect his clothing, which he would call for later. On April 3, 1934, Green, accompanied by his wife Beth, drove up to the maids' home. As soon as he reached the front door, he could tell from one of the women's behavior that something was amiss. He quickly turned and ran towards his car, but federal officers who were lying in wait opened fire. Green never made it down the walkway. He died in hospital eight days later.

Following Little Bohemia, the new Dillinger Gang had all but parted company, the fates awaiting these renegade outlaws as equally unpleasant as those of their predecessors.

Wheelman Tommy Carroll was next, his demise occurring on June 5, 1934. He and his wife Jean were casing banks in Iowa and had stopped in Waterloo to have some repair work done to their car. While the work was being done, they left the garage for a few minutes, and the mechanic just happened to notice a machine gun poorly concealed by a lap robe in the backseat. He immediately called the police, who were waiting when Carroll and his wife returned to the garage. Carroll didn't even wait for the order to surrender before pulling a gun. The two officers fired, killing him instantly.

Death was a part of the profession; every gangster knew it. But Dillinger was particularly incensed at the shooting of Carroll, who was well liked by the gang. With uncharacteristic fury, he said, "We'll have to pay a visit to Waterloo and take care of those cops."

Homer Van Meter, to whom he was venting his anger, replied, "If we spend all our time 'taking care' of people, we won't have any time left for robbing banks."

Little time was left for Van Meter at any rate. The gangster had found himself in a bad way after July 22. Upon hearing that Dillinger (or his double) had been betrayed, Van Meter knew that he was in jeopardy, so he left Chicago for St. Paul the night of the Biograph shooting.

Although Van Meter knew he was safe in St. Paul provided he kept himself under wraps, he was suffocating both from inactivity and the relentless pressure applied to his "protectors" by federal, state and local police in their intense search for the remaining public enemies. All of a sudden everyone seemed to be falling, and Van Meter knew that he could easily be next.

But he could scarcely expect that his own betrayal would come at the hands of a colleague. A long-standing feud likely paved the way for Homer Van Meter's demise. Baby Face Nelson and Van Meter had detested each other right from the start. Van Meter's loyalty to Dillinger both humiliated and incensed the volatile Nelson, and it was only Dillinger's calming influence that prevented many a bloody gunfight.

Dillinger once said that if ever given the chance, one of the two would kill the other. But perhaps the more easygoing Van Meter forgot about their rivalry in view of his other concerns. Nelson was of a different temperament, however, and neither forgot nor forgave. When his manic fury wasn't released through robberies or random killings, he had plenty of time to let past grievances fester.

It was Nelson's nature to gun for his enemies. But Baby Face had also ascended to the rank of Public Enemy Number One in the wake of Dillinger's alleged death, or…disappearance. And, although psychotic, the gangster wasn't deluded enough to risk apprehension merely to satisfy a personal grudge; he knew that Van Meter was a man to be reckoned with. The lanky, sleepy-eyed outlaw may have had the appearance of a bumpkin, but Homer Van Meter was both quick and deadly on the draw. And so, apparently, Nelson devised another plan.

Van Meter realized that with Dillinger and the other A-1 gangsters gone and most of the others working as independents or divided into splinter groups, the heyday of his criminal career had passed. But he still tried to capitalize on his former glory and openly offered his services to lesser outfits in exchange for protection and security. But Van Meter's reputation, which continued to interest the police, at first brought no takers from the underworld.

Van Meter was despondent. Then, on the evening of Sunday, August 23, 1934, a minor-league burglary gang contacted him. They were apparently excited about having a man of Van Meter's stature join them. Van Meter, although downplaying his enthusiasm, was delighted. He threw on a hat and other outer garments to conceal his appearance and hurried towards the meeting place.

Suddenly, a police car intercepted him at the corner of University Avenue and Marion Street. The police ordered Van Meter to surrender. But the impulsive gangster drew his gun instead and ran towards an alley where, cornered, he turned to face his pursuers, who blew him apart with relentless blasts of machine-gun fire.

Whether it truly was Baby Face Nelson who'd informed on his former colleague, ironically yet conveniently effecting his vengeance through the intervention of the law, the pint-sized gangster was now the last member of the Dillinger Gang still at large. He had become the most wanted man in America.

Whereas Dillinger had to be taken down because of his cocky, spit-in-the-eye attitude towards the law in general and the FBI in particular, Nelson was a true Public Enemy, eclipsing even the cinematic bad-guy exploits of Edward G. Robinson and James Cagney.

He was the renegade gunman of the Dillinger outfit, who hated cops even more than Dillinger and made a point of showing it. He'd already graphically demonstrated his contempt for the FBI by his merciless killing of Special Agent W. Carter Baum. And not one of the agents assigned to track down the mad-dog killer kidded himself into believing that Baby Face Nelson would ever be taken alive.

❧⠀❧

CHAPTER THREE

Baby Face Nelson
(1908–1934)

"It was just like Jimmy Cagney!"

–A witness describing Baby Face Nelson's final shootout with FBI agents

ALONG WITH CLYDE BARROW, Baby Face Nelson earned a reputation as the most ruthless killer in Depression Day America. There were similarities between the two. Both Barrow and Nelson were slight of build, possessing peach-smooth, pleasant features that belied their true psychopathic natures. Both had a pathological attachment to their weapons (Clyde preferred handguns and the Browning automatic; Nelson favored the tommy gun), and each had no reservation about using them on anyone who got in his way.

Yet, unlike Barrow, Nelson's family life presented an interesting contradiction to his amoral behavior. According to Alvin Karpis, although Baby Face Nelson would "endure some bullet-punctured years ahead," the Lester Gillis he knew was a devoted husband and father who enjoyed spending time with his loving wife, Helen, and their two children.

Karpis had taken meals with the Gillis clan on occasion and recalled, "They were a pleasant family."

Lester M. Gillis, aka Baby Face Nelson, once described as having the face of an angel and the soul of the devil

～✕～

Karpis also speculated that the only reason Nelson got his "mad-dog" reputation was because the authorities wouldn't leave him alone on an earlier rap, and when he finally pushed back, he fought hard. Hard indeed. By the time Baby Face Nelson's reign of terror came to an end, he had killed at least six people, three of whom were FBI agents.

He was nicknamed "Baby Face" because even at the time of his death, at age 26, he looked like a teenager. Yet no one, not even his criminal cronies, dared to call him by that name. Much as Al Capone despised "Scarface," and Benjamin Siegel loathed "Bugsy," the moniker "Baby Face" could provoke a violent response from the mercurial Nelson.

To compensate for his youthful looks and detested small stature, as his reputation grew, Nelson insisted on being called "Big George" Nelson. Not surprisingly, the name was hardly taken seriously by his underworld associates. Or by anyone else for that matter.

Nelson had to rely on his fearless reputation and boundless ferocity to earn him the respect and recognition he so desperately sought. It was through an insatiable murderous appetite that he achieved his goal. Nearly seven decades after his death, the name Baby Face Nelson remains synonymous with the unrestrained violence of the era.

Lester Joseph Gillis was born on Chicago's southwest side on December 6, 1908. He was the youngest of six children: four daughters and another son, each of whom grew up to lead respectable lives. His parents, Josef and Mary Gillis, were Belgian immigrants who had a difficult time adapting to life in America. Josef worked as an unskilled laborer at the Union Stockyards, where he put in long days for little money. Like many other immigrants who had come to the U.S. seeking a better way of life, he was disillusioned not to be living the American Dream.

Because of the arduous 12-hour, 6-day workweek, Josef had little time to spend with his family. Mary Gillis was left to raise the children almost on her own. As a result, Lester took to the streets early, having developed a bitterness, both at his family's economic want and at his own short stature. His delicate features and 5'4" frame made him a prime target for bullies on the prowl seeking ways to vent their own impoverished frustrations. They took delight in beating young Lester with everything from fists to blackjacks and bricks. Even his friends, who grew proportionately for their ages, began to snub the one they called "the little runt."

Lester knew that in order to survive the hellish environment, he would have to learn to fight back. And fight back he did. Aggressively. Where previously he had been a passive punching bag, inwardly seething but doing little to defend himself, Lester now returned punches. If threatened or challenged, Lester followed the unspoken rules of street fighting and hit back with any weapon at his disposal.

As his reputation for toughness grew, it was Lester who often took on the bully role, instigating fights that he would quickly finish. Eventually, he became the leader of the gang of hooligans who used to torment him but now regarded him with respect. He could walk his neighborhood confidently, without fear. A mere look from Lester Gillis often sent other kids scurrying away.

Lester, however, was eager to advance his standing beyond the mere awe of his peers. He and his gang embarked on a Dead End Kid crime spree involving vandalism, muggings and petty thievery. Lester succeeded not only in forging a reputation on the street, but with the local police as well.

At the age of 14, Lester left school and spent more time on street corners cultivating his tough guy image. In 1922, Lester crossed the line into grand larceny when he stole a car. He was arrested and sent to the St. Charles Reform School.

His almost two years at the boys' home provided him with a learning experience of the worst possible kind. Although his mother later claimed that her son's behavior was "exemplary," reformatory officials labeled Lester "incorrigible." He took delight in bullying the other boys and showed a chronic disrespect for authority. He responded with indifference or with sneering contempt to the harsh discipline that was often inflicted upon him.

When he was released from St. Charles, Lester hadn't the faintest desire to rehabilitate himself, so he immediately returned to the street, resuming his delinquent ways. His record of juvenile offenses continued to grow. Five months after his release from St. Charles, police discovered him breaking into a department store. He cursed and struggled as they tried to pull his tiny but agile form from the window well. He was soon overcome and taken before a judge.

Because Lester's innocent features stood in such striking contrast to his miscreant behavior pattern, the magistrate was initially sympathetic to his predicament. But Lester neither expected nor wanted special treatment and let the magistrate know it.

"You can just go to hell!" he spat at the judge.

Lester's outburst stiffened the judge's demeanor, and he sentenced the youth to the maximum of two years at the Chicago Boy's Home.

Lester emerged from this second stint with a warped view of life and the world in general. He left the reformatory with the same burning bitterness John Dillinger felt on his release from Michigan City. But while Dillinger maintained some vestige of humanity in his criminal pursuits, Lester Gillis wanted to strike back at society with a brutal vengeance.

Prohibition was in full swing when Lester was released in 1926. Through Al Capone's efforts, Chicago had become the hub of criminal activity in the U.S., and Lester desperately wanted to become involved in some facet of the bootleg industry since it apparently offered both easy money and, more importantly, protection.

But the racketeers considered him a nobody. Having spent almost four consecutive years behind reformatory walls, Lester had to find some way to prove himself to the criminal elite.

With no connections and little capital, Lester decided that his best bet was in selling protection, where just threat and muscle could pull in big coin. He hooked up with some of his old gang and began harassing pawnshops, brothels and bookie joints. It was because of his efficiency in the protection racket that Capone's top triggerman "Machine Gun" Jack McGurn finally approached him.

Capone had appointed McGurn to recruit tough guys who could be "persuasive" in labor relations, an area where Scarface had some influence. Lester became an enforcer, and he reveled in his work, particularly when he was required to back up his arguments with force. Lester's strong-arm tactics, although effective, occasionally took on near-homicidal brutality, and when the labor bosses started complaining, Capone instructed McGurn to drop him from the payroll.

Lester was livid as a result of his dismissal, but he knew better than to stand up to Capone. Without a steady cash flow he soon found himself in dire straits, so he turned his talents to armed robbery.

Lester's personal life also took a turn when he found romance with 16-year-old Helen Warwick (shortened from Wawrzyniak) whom he married in Indiana in June 1928. She'd met Lester while working behind the hardware counter at a downtown Woolworth's and later recalled how she was instantly charmed by him.

Yearning for a more exciting life, Helen willingly supported his criminal lifestyle. At the same time, they both wanted children, and 10 months after their marriage, their son Ronald was born, followed by daughter Darlene 10 months later.

While possessed of a wild and murderous temperament in his professional undertakings, Lester enjoyed the domesticity of family life. He took his role as husband and father seriously, so to provide for his family, he held up several stores in the Chicago area. He was clearly a novice in his new trade, and

none of his scores was impressive. Yet, with Helen's encouragement, he kept at it, convincing himself that he would soon
strike it big. Christmas came early for the Gillises in late 1930,
when Lester robbed a prosperous Wheaton, Illinois, gem dealer
of over $5000.

"They say there's a Depression going on in this country?" he
chimed as he slipped a diamond engagement ring onto
Helen's finger. "Now you're really my 'Million Dollar Baby
from a Five and Ten Cent Store'" (a nickname Lester had
coined for his wife from a popular song of the day).

Heady with success, Lester next hit a jewelry store in
Chicago on January 15, 1931. The heist went off smoothly, but
just days later the Chicago police arrested him. Now branded
a "three-time loser," Lester was given a sentence of one year to
life for the robbery with time to be served at the State Penitentiary at Joliet.

Things looked even bleaker for Lester Gillis (Inmate #5437)
when a witness identified him as the lone gunman who had
robbed the gem dealer in Wheaton. At age 23, Lester Gillis was
looking at spending the rest of his life behind bars.

Helen Gillis' devotion to her husband never wavered. She
visited him frequently and may even have acted as the getaway
driver for his escape. On February 17, 1932, Lester was returning
to Joliet by commuter train following his postponed pretrial
hearing in Wheaton, when he attacked the plainclothes detective accompanying him and jumped from the train into a
waiting sedan.

Lester high-tailed it to California, where he apparently came
under the protection of Sicilian mob boss Giuseppe (Joe) Parente. Parente, impressed by Lester's past association with
Capone, put him to work in several capacities that best utilized
his skills. He served as bodyguard, driver, safecracker and gunman. Unfortunately for Lester's enormous ego, he also per-
formed such menial duties as bartender and parking valet.

Because he did whatever Parente assigned him without complaint (at least not in earshot of the crime boss), Lester was eventually promoted to bootlegger. He also adopted the alias "George Nelson," after a prizefighter he admired, and he insisted on being called by that name.

Nelson's work as a bootlegger consisted of enforcing the sale of Parente's liquor to speakeasies, primarily in the Sausilito area. His approach to "speak" owners was reminiscent of Jimmy Cagney's aggressive sales delivery in the classic gangster movie *The Public Enemy.* Nelson used whatever tactics were necessary, from uttering threats against the man's wife and family to what he most enjoyed, employing a little muscle or firearm persuasion. He met with little resistance from his customers.

Often accompanying Nelson on these "sales calls" was Parente's errand boy, John Paul Chase. Chase didn't have enough smarts to achieve personal advancement in the Parente organization, but he teamed well with Nelson, and although he was seven years older than his pal, Chase grew to idolize him.

Parente continued to humiliate Nelson with demeaning tasks and had even begun introducing him to his Sicilian compatriots as "Baby Face" Nelson. Nelson was not a man to be humbled, even by a gang boss as powerful as Parente, so he finally decided to quit the organization and work independently. John Paul Chase also left Parente to become Nelson's partner.

Two other Parente gunmen chose to team up with Nelson: Tommy Carroll and Eddie Green (known in underworld parlance as a "jugmarker"—the man who picked and scouted banks for robbery). Both had pulled bank jobs throughout the Midwest, and Nelson and Chase sat enthralled listening to their exploits of near escapes and fast getaways.

Carroll and Green said that banks in the prairie states were ripe for the picking. And so Nelson, Chase and the ever-faithful

Helen packed up their belongings and headed for the Midwest. They began their bank-robbing career in earnest, hitting banks in Iowa, Nebraska and Wisconsin throughout the fall and winter of 1933.

While Nelson was pleased with the take from these jobs, his ego suffered because his efforts were being credited to either John Dillinger or Pretty Boy Floyd, both of whom had already established their reputations. In frustration, Nelson drove to Long Beach, Indiana, to seek out Homer Van Meter, who was recently paroled from Michigan City. Nelson figured that, through Van Meter, he might set up a meeting with Dillinger.

Van Meter took an instant dislike to Nelson.

"Johnny doesn't work with punks," Van Meter told him bluntly.

Nelson held the reins on his temper.

"I'm no punk, an' I don't like to be called one," he replied. "I've hit banks all across three states."

"That so?" Van Meter said, unimpressed.

"Only I don't get no credit for the jobs I pull," Nelson complained to him.

Van Meter smirked. "Maybe there's a reason for that. Come back and see us when you're all grown up, Baby Face."

Nelson displayed remarkable restraint. He felt so vilified that he could have shot Van Meter dead on the spot. It sparked the beginning of a mutual loathing and distrust between the pair that within months had tragic consequences for Homer Van Meter. But Nelson knew that killing Van Meter wouldn't endear him to Dillinger, so as he stormed out the room, he again decided to establish his own reputation.

The Baby Face Nelson Gang hit fast and pulled no punches. Nelson learned a lot by watching Tommy Carroll and Eddie Green in action. They'd sweep into a bank with machine guns blazing towards the ceiling, and while everyone was cowering on the floor, they'd scoop up the money from the cash drawers and the vault, then spray the walls with gunfire to announce their getaway.

The distinctive shoot-'em-up style of Nelson's bank jobs soon gave his gang its own identity. His name finally became known, but he was not completely flattered by the publicity. Reporters had somehow discovered his hated nickname, and until the end of his life, the former Lester Gillis was pegged in the press as "Baby Face."

Nelson and pal John Paul Chase temporarily parted company when the latter returned to California to visit relatives. Nelson decided to take a vacation, so he and Helen headed to St. Paul, Minnesota.

Life was good for Nelson. He and Helen lived in luxurious surroundings at the St. Francis Hotel. Gangsters could feel secure in St. Paul because the police protected them provided they didn't cause any trouble. During the 1930s, the St. Paul Police Department was one of the most corrupt in America.

It was in St. Paul that Nelson got a surprise visit from Homer Van Meter. Accompanied by John Hamilton, Van Meter came right to the point. He needed manpower to assemble a new gang. With Harry Pierpont, Charles Makley, Russell Clark and Dillinger all in custody, only he and Hamilton were still at large.

"Johnny'll be out soon, I can tell ya that," Van Meter added. "But we're gonna need some big action."

Nelson was pleased to be in the driver's seat. He calmly outlined the upcoming scores his gang had planned: Sioux Falls, South Dakota, and Mason City, Iowa. Then he added, "Can Dillinger take orders?"

Both Van Meter and Hamilton were shocked speechless. Hamilton started to swear, but Van Meter hushed him.

"Johnny'll go along with it," he said.

Two weeks later, Dillinger escaped from Crown Point and hooked up with his new associates in St. Paul. He met with

Nelson in his suite at the St. Francis along with Homer Van Meter, John Hamilton, Tommy Carroll and Eddie Green. Dillinger tried to be cordial, but Nelson was abrupt. He made it clear that he would give the orders and then outlined his procedure for robbing a bank.

"I walk in, start shooting and kill everything that moves."

Dillinger sat quietly, his eyes focused on the little gangster.

Van Meter was furious. He realized that he had made a grave mistake bringing this bantam psychotic into the gang, and he let Nelson know exactly what he thought of his planning. As the two launched into the first of many confrontations, it was left to Dillinger to cool the tempers in the room.

"Fellas," he said calmly, "if we're gonna work together, we've gotta keep our heads about us." But Dillinger had gotten his first glimpse into the unstable personality of Baby Face Nelson.

The following day, Dillinger experienced a more graphic display of Nelson's temperament. Nelson was driving Dillinger across town to pick up Van Meter, when he ran a stop sign and rammed into another car at the intersection. The driver, Theodore Kidder, was uninjured but furious. He jumped from his car and headed towards Nelson. Before Dillinger could stop him, Nelson drew his .45 from his coat and calmly shot Kidder right between the eyes.

As Nelson threw the car into reverse and drove off, Dillinger chastised him. "You didn't have to do that?"

Nelson was unapologetic. "Hell, yes! He recognized you."

"Well, a citizen back there got your license number," Dillinger pointed out.

Nelson began cursing so wildly he almost lost control of the car a second time.

Nelson's next insane outburst occurred on March 6, 1934, when he, Dillinger, Van Meter, Hamilton, Green and Carroll hit the Securities National Bank and Trust Company in Sioux Falls, South Dakota.

Tommy Carroll waited behind the wheel of the stolen Packard while the other gang members walked through the doors of the bank just before closing time. Dillinger led them with his Thompson submachine gun at the ready.

Dillinger and Van Meter quickly lined up the employees and covered them while Nelson scooped up the cash from the tellers' cages. Hamilton came out and reported that the door to the vault was locked.

"Someone get that safe open," Dillinger ordered. "Who knows the combination?"

When no one volunteered, Dillinger grew impatient. He threatened to shoot the lot of them unless someone spoke up. Finally, employees pointed to a trembling middle-aged man. Dillinger persuaded him with a hard kick to the butt to open the safe.

Suddenly, the bank security alarm sounded. Nelson burst into a rage, screaming: "Which one of you did that? I'll kill the son of a bitch who hit that alarm!"

"Never mind that," Dillinger said. "Just keep an eye out for the cops."

Nelson scowled at Dillinger. He was supposed to be running the show. Moments later, Nelson saw off-duty police officer Hale Keith getting out of a car. Nelson opened fire through the plate-glass window, and the wounded Keith fell to the pavement.

Nelson cheered his own accomplishment. "I got one of 'em!" he squealed.

Because of Nelson's eager trigger finger, the gang was forced to rush their robbery and make a quick getaway. Despite their haste, they were pleased with the take, which amounted to $49,000. But Dillinger had serious concerns about Nelson. It was bad business to shoot a policeman, and the gangster had done it as casually as if he was shooting tin cans off a fence. Dillinger would have preferred to break company with Nelson then and there, but he was an honorable thief and would not betray even a loony like Nelson when he and his pals were benefiting from Nelson's scores.

On March 13, eight days after Sioux Falls, the gang struck at the First National Bank in Mason City, Iowa. Eddie Green, the "jugmarker," discovered that the bank's vault held more than $240,000 in currency. What neither Green nor anyone else realized was that, unlike many of the "sardine cans" the gang had opened, this institution had taken special precautions to protect its customers' money.

Bank President Willis Bagley anticipated trouble from the moment he saw the suspicious group enter the premises. He locked himself in his office while Homer Van Meter fired shots futilely at the door.

From inside a specially equipped steel cage above the lobby, bank guard Tom Walters tossed a teargas shell at Eddie Green, striking him on the back. Enraged, Green whirled around and fired a volley at the cage, but the bullets were ineffective against the reinforced metal.

A stinging cloud of tear gas wafted through the lobby, burning the outlaws' eyes and blurring their vision. But they were determined to finish what they'd started, so they placed handkerchiefs over their mouths and noses as they continued to empty out the tellers' cash drawers.

John Hamilton was facing his own frustration. Since the bank president had the vault key and was safely ensconced in his office, Hamilton was forced to order cashier Harry Fisher at gunpoint to pass stacks of money through the locked, barred doorway of the vault. Fisher complied but began handing out stacks of one-dollar bills.

Baby Face Nelson, as the lookout, was chain-smoking and pacing away his nervous energy on the street in front of the bank. Suddenly, a female bank customer came rushing up to him from the alley.

"Mister, please—" she sputtered breathlessly. "Get the police. The bank is being held up."

"Lady, you're telling me?" Nelson replied, indicating his machine gun.

Dillinger, nearly overcome with teargas fumes, stumbled from the bank towards Nelson. At that moment, a shot rang out from across the street, grazing Dillinger's elbow. Dillinger returned fire with a burst from his machine gun then yelled to Van Meter that they were getting out.

Van Meter rushed back into the bank to get Hamilton, who was becoming increasingly aggravated with the slow progress of cashier Harry Fisher. Van Meter insisted that they leave, and Hamilton reluctantly complied, aware that his money sack contained only a small percentage of what he could see behind the bars of the vault.

Dillinger knew that as each second ticked by, their chance to escape narrowed. Nelson didn't care; he was pumped for battle. But the crafty Dillinger came up with a better plan, one intended to avoid bloodshed. Rushing back into the foyer of the bank, he and Van Meter began herding out hostages. Dillinger thought that the plan would not only guarantee them protection from the police, but also from the sniper who was apparently still in position somewhere across the street.

The sniper, an elderly policeman named John Shipley, managed to get off another shot from the window of his third-floor office, this one catching John Hamilton in the shoulder.

Dillinger and the others jumped into their Buick, which they surrounded with more than 20 hostages poised on the running boards, fenders and back bumpers. It was a comical sight, like something out of the Keystone Cops, but Police Chief E. J. Patton found nothing funny in the mocking, 25-mile-per-hour getaway Dillinger and his gang executed in his town.

Neither did Nelson who, perhaps because his taste for blood hadn't been satisfied on this job, began harassing one of the hostages, an elderly man who happened to be the bank vice president. Nelson wouldn't let up, and it appeared that he was just waiting for a wrong word from the old man so he could plug him. Finally, Nelson pushed the man to the point where the senior called him a son of a bitch, and Nelson glee-fully pulled his gun. Just as Nelson fired, someone knocked the gun from his hand, and the bullet plunged harmlessly into the car door.

Dillinger, seated in the back, said sternly, "He's a harmless old man, Nelson. Now let's stop this goddamn nonsense and get outta here."

The Buick rolled out of Mason City, and five miles from town the gangsters released the hostages unharmed. For their efforts, Dillinger and his gang netted a mere $52,000, which was far below their anticipated take.

The FBI's newly established list of the nation's Public Ene-mies included John Dillinger at Number 1 and George "Baby Face" Nelson at Number 21. Names soon to be forgotten in the annals of crime preceded Nelson's, and he was more deter-mined than ever to do something about it.

"Don't those lawmen know they're dealing with the most dangerous man in America?" Nelson fumed.

But the list was compiled by the Bureau's Chicago office in December 1933, and already Nelson had made significant inroads to improve his status.

After Mason City, the gang took off in separate directions. Dillinger was traced to St. Paul, where he was almost cornered at the Lincoln Court Apartments. But thanks to Homer Van Meter, Dillinger escaped with only a slight bullet wound to his leg.

The heat was on, and Dillinger decided the gang needed to cool off and plan its next move. He chose a fishing resort on the shores of Spider Lake, called Little Bohemia Lodge. Nelson and wife Helen fled to the woodlands of Iron County, Wisconsin, to await word on where to rejoin the others. The only member of the "new" Dillinger Gang who did not make the rendezvous was Eddie Green because he fell under a barrage of federal bullets on April 3, 1934.

It was early afternoon on April 20 that the gang reconnected at the resort, which was perfect for their needs given its remote location and off-season promise of privacy. Nelson came with his wife, and each of the other men (excluding Dillinger and a hanger-on named Pat Reilly) brought along his girlfriend.

Emil Wanatka was the proprietor of the large resort. He welcomed his 10 guests, pleased that he could entertain some business during his slow season. But he and his wife were suspicious of why these city folk would choose this time of the year to vacation at his lodge.

The gang gave Wanatka no cause for concern. The three days they enjoyed at the two-story lodge were spent playing cards, going for walks through the woods and eating Mrs. Wanatka's fine home cooking.

The Wanatkas soon came to the conclusion that their guests were the infamous Dillinger Gang, and they secretly contacted the authorities. The ensuing shootout at Little Bohemia, carried out under the direction of Special Agent Melvin Purvis, was a complete debacle and tarnished the image of the FBI. Dillinger and his gang managed to slip away using a previously planned escape route. All the federal agents got for their trouble were the gangsters' female companions and public outrage over their shooting of three innocent lodge guests, one of whom died from his wounds.

Baby Face Nelson was in his cottage sleeping with his wife when the melee began.

"I'm gonna have to park you, doll," he said to his wife, as he quickly tossed on his clothes. "Things might be rough for a while, but you'll be all right."

"You just take care of yourself, Lester," Helen begged him.

There was no back exit from the cabin, so Nelson burst out the front door, firing a pair of automatics. He briefly exchanged shots with the machine-gun-toting Purvis, and one of Nelson's bullets narrowly missed the G-man's skull.

Either by choice or in confusion, Nelson ran in the opposite direction from the other gangsters, getting lost in the dense woodlands. As he moved deeper into the forest, he could hear the distant voices of FBI agents as they scoured the woods for the outlaws. He came upon a clearing bordered by several small fishing cabins—a place called Koerner's Resort. He desperately needed a vehicle and spotted a car, which thankfully had keys dangling in the ignition.

Nelson hurriedly slid behind the wheel. Before he could turn over the engine, a pair of bright headlights shone in his face. Nelson waited until the approaching vehicle came to a stop, then leaped out and ran towards the car.

Before the shooting started, Purvis had dispatched special Agents J.C. Newman and W. Carter Baum to phone for reinforcements. Also in the car was their driver, Deputy Constable Carl Christensen. None of the men had expected to run head-long into Baby Face Nelson.

"Awright, get outta the car," Nelson ordered.

W. Carter Baun responded, "We're federal agents."

Nelson shouted, "I know who you are. I also know you bastards wear bulletproof vests, so I'll give it to you high and low!"

The men never had a chance. Before they could draw their weapons, Nelson emptied both .45s into them, killing the two agents; W. Carter Baum died from a bullet to the head. Nelson removed their dead and dying bodies and drove off in the constable's coupe.

Nelson stayed out of sight for the next several days, hiding out at the Indian reservation at Lac du Flambeau. When the food supply ran low and Nelson was reduced to eating lard,

A familiar sight during the era of the public enemy was the distribution and displaying of wanted posters, which were often affixed to post office walls. Because of newsreels and the popular series *Crime Does Not Pay*, the dour faces of the era's gangsters became entrenched in the public consciousness. Most criminals despised the publicity, but Baby Face Nelson was an exception. He liked to have his face and reputation acknowledged. The egomaniacal gangster especially resented that the reward posted for his capture was half that offered for John Dillinger. Even after Dillinger's "death," Baby Face was regarded as a second-rate hoodlum.

he left the reserve, stole a car belonging to a mail carrier and drove to Chicago, where he reunited with his wife. Helen had been taken into police custody following the raid on Little Bohemia but was released soon after.

Nelson's immense ego was again bruised when he learned that even after killing an FBI agent, the bounty on his head was only half the $20,000 offered for Dillinger. Nelson was so enraged that he swore to rob a bank a day for a month!

His murderous handiwork had, however, elevated Baby Face Nelson to number two on the FBI's most wanted list, so Nelson and Helen drove to California to wait for things to cool off. There, Nelson reconnected with pal John Paul Chase and began making plans to put together a new gang.

But the tide was turning. Federal officers were winning the war against crime in the Midwest. Their crowning achievement came on July 22, 1934, when the FBI shot John Dillinger (or his decoy) outside the Biograph Theater.

Nelson never disliked Dillinger, only envied his status both among the police and the underworld. And with "the big shot" out of the way, Nelson quickly inherited the title of Public Enemy Number One. He may not have been recognized as "Big George" Nelson, but the entire nation knew the sobriquet "Baby Face" Nelson.

The Nelsons and John Paul Chase remained in California throughout the summer of 1934. By the time August rolled around, Nelson's hopes to assemble his own gang were dashed. Eddie Green was dead, as were Tommy Carroll, John Hamilton and Homer Van Meter, although Nelson hardly shed a tear over the latter's demise. Most of the veterans were either dead, in jail or on the run. And with the FBI applying a tight stranglehold on crime, Nelson couldn't see a lot of new talent on the horizon.

Nelson even tried to reestablish himself with his old organized crime associates, but they wanted nothing to do with a maverick killer saddled with the tag Public Enemy Number One. With only his wife and John Paul Chase at his side, Nelson made the crazy decision to return to the Midwest, the territory where he was most sought.

FBI Inspector Samuel Cowley, one of the agents who had been stationed outside the Biograph Theater on the night of July 22, now focused all his energies on capturing Baby Face Nelson. On learning that the gangster had returned to his old stomping grounds, Cowley put his department on 24-hour alert and ordered surveillance of all main and back roads between Chicago and Lake Geneva, Wisconsin, where eyewitnesses reported seeing Nelson. Following the tragic misfire at Little Bohemia, Cowley was determined not to let Nelson get away again.

But Nelson was keeping an uncharacteristically low profile. He was concerned less for himself than for loyal Helen, who once commented how handsome her husband looked "cradling a machine gun under his arm."

For several weeks, the trio moved around and somehow managed to avoid being spotted by vigilant G-men who patrolled every main route and gravel road and regularly checked out diners and filling stations. It had been Nelson's plan to rent a cottage near Lake Geneva for the upcoming winter, but the FBI learned of his intentions and took up armed positions inside the house of his prospective host.

As Nelson drove onto the property, an overeager agent stepped out onto the porch. Nelson instantly knew that it was a setup, and he slammed his Ford V8 into reverse, squealing into a 180° spin and darting away from the potential ambush.

Heading southeast towards Chicago, about 75 miles away, Nelson and his companions were spotted by Special Agents William Ryan and Thomas McDade, who immediately spun their car around and took off in pursuit. Nelson didn't like being hunted, and after a brief chase, he unexpectedly whipped his Ford into a screeching turn so that he was now pursuing the federal car. The agents drove faster but so did Nelson, racing alongside their vehicle so that John Paul Chase, who was in the back seat, could shoot at them with his automatic rifle.

For several miles the two cars exchanged fire in a running gun battle, until a bullet finally punctured the fuel pump of Nelson's car. McDade and Ryan decided not to attempt apprehension, but instead zoomed off farther down the road, where they abandoned their vehicle and concealed themselves in the tall grass in preparation to ambush the faltering V8. But once they drove away, a second car carrying Samuel Cowley and Special Agent Herman Hollis joined the pursuit.

Nelson's car finally stalled, and the three occupants exited hastily. As Helen Gillis sought protection in a ditch, Baby Face and Chase collected their weapons and took up position beside the Ford. Agents Cowley and Hollis, armed with a Thompson submachine gun and shotgun respectively, jumped out of their car and likewise crouched behind it for cover. The gun battle raged for several minutes before Nelson, growing impatient, rose from behind his car.

Chase was incredulous. "What the hell are you doin', Les?"

"I've had enough of this cat and mouse," he replied and then proceeded forward, firing his machine gun continuously without letup.

Agent Hollis pumped rounds from his shotgun into Nelson's legs until his ammo was exhausted. Then he pulled out his pistol and, still firing, dashed towards a nearby telephone pole. Nelson pivoted his machine gun towards him, and Hollis fell dead with a bullet in his brain.

Cowley continued to return fire, but no matter how much damage he inflicted upon Nelson, the little gangster kept coming. Cowley was hit several times, yet managed to keep firing until he finally lost consciousness.

Nelson was shot 17 times. He staggered towards the agents' car, as Helen and Chase joined him.

"You'll have to drive, I'm hit," was all he said.

The next day an anonymous telephone call led police and federal agents to St. Paul's Cemetery where Nelson's nude, bullet-riddled corpse was discovered. Apparently, he had lived for several hours.

When he finally expired, a distraught Helen Gillis said, "My pal is gone."

Special Agent Samuel Cowley, 35 years old and proclaimed a "shining star" by the Bureau, was rushed to the hospital but also died within a few hours.

Helen Gillis was arrested shortly afterwards and sentenced to a year in the federal prison at Milan, Michigan, for harboring her fugitive husband. Upon her release, she disappeared from the public eye.

John Paul Chase returned to California where he managed to elude the law until December 24, 1934, when federal agents found him in the custody of the Mount Shasta police. He was tried for murder and sentenced to life imprisonment at Alcatraz. Paroled in 1966, he died of cancer in Palo Alto, California, on October 5, 1973.

According to Nelson's widow, in his dying hours, Baby Face had reportedly said to Chase, "Drop everything and get me to a priest."

It seems the ultimate irony that a man who cared so little for human life should seek religious solace in his last hours. Yet, perhaps God in his mercy accepted his deathbed conversion. But the rest of society breathed a sigh of relief to finally be rid of Baby Face Nelson.

CHAPTER FOUR

Pretty Boy Floyd
(1904–1934)

"I guess I've been accused of everything that has happened except the kidnapping of the Lindbergh child."

–Charles Arthur "Pretty Boy" Floyd

PRETTY BOY FLOYD was either one of the coldest killers of the Depression era, ranking up with Clyde Barrow and Baby Face Nelson for sheer murderous audacity, or the most unfairly maligned. It is true that when cornered, Floyd used firepower to make his getaways. Records show that he shot his way out of more scrapes than most desperadoes, with the possible exception of Bonnie and Clyde. But those who knew Floyd swore that his basic country bumpkin persona would never have lent itself to participation in one of the bloodiest days in the history of American crime: the Kansas City Massacre, where gangsters machine-gunned down five men, including three law officers and a federal agent who never had the chance to defend themselves. Up until the moment that he took his final breath in an Ohio cornfield on October 22 at 4:25 PM, Floyd swore he was innocent of any complicity in the massacre.

Yet a man who bore a striking resemblance to the muscular 6'2" Floyd was identified at the scene. And because of Floyd's quick-draw reputation and that he'd long sought refuge amid the political corruption in Kansas City, Missouri, officials promptly tagged Pretty Boy Floyd as the chief gunman. The press took it from there, and before long Charles Arthur Floyd, Okie desperado, had become the most wanted man in America.

There are no apologies for Pretty Boy Floyd, but he was something of an anomaly. While he wouldn't hesitate to shoot down an interfering police officer (Dillinger once said of Floyd: "That bird's too quick on the trigger."), he was basically a simple hill-bred man possessed of a charm and gentility best exemplified in his relationship with his wife Ruby and son Dempsey.

Others who knew "Choc" Floyd remember not an infamous public enemy, but a folk hero, a "bucolic bandit," whose criminal exploits were motivated as much by a desire to help neighbors driven to ruin by heartless bankers as they were to obtain personal wealth. To his people, he was the "Robin Hood of Cookson Hills."

In the years following his death he became the most sympathetic of the Depression Day gangsters. In 1939, Pretty Boy Floyd achieved literary immortality in John Steinbeck's Pulitzer prize-winning novel *The Grapes of Wrath*. At one point in the book, the character of Ma Joad speaks about the conditions of the time and Floyd's inevitable descent into crime.

> *I knowed Purty Boy Floyd…I knowed his Ma. They was good folks. He was full of hell, sure, like a good boy oughta be…He done a little bad thing an' they hurt him, caught 'im and hurt 'im so he was mad an' the next bad thing he done was mad, an' they hurt 'im again. An' purty soon he was mean-mad.*
>
> *They shot at him like a varmint, an' he shot back, an' they run 'im like a coyote, an' him a-snappin' an' a-snarlin', mean as a lobo. An' he was mad. He wasn't no boy or no man no more, he was jus' a walkin' chunk of mean-mad.*

For a man destined to achieve such widespread notoriety, Charles Arthur Floyd's beginnings were less than humble. He was born February 3, 1904, in northwest Georgia, the fourth child and second son of Walter Lee and Mamie Helena Echols Floyd. In 1911, when Charley was seven, his family, looking to make a new start, packed up their belongings and eventually settled in Sequoyah County in mid-eastern Oklahoma.

Walter and Mamie were discouraged in their attempts to find a better life for the family and were soon forced to endure the hardship of toiling on the land. Working long, grueling hours, Walter and young Charley barely eked out a living for the family in their attempts to grow food and cash crops, all the while running a race against the dust storms and soil erosion that seemed to endlessly threaten their meager livelihood. It was a monotonous, frustrating and unfulfilling existence, especially for a boy of Charley's curiosity and adventurous spirit.

Eventually, he was forced to quit school to help on the farm full time. But at day's end Charley, would immerse himself in the exploits of famous Western bad men, such as the James Brothers and the Daltons who, during their outlaw reign, spent time in the Oklahoma hills and who may have even walked on the land where Charley was growing cotton and corn.

Jesse James was Charley's particular fascination. Besides reading dime-store novels by the score, he occasionally ran into an old-timer who claimed to have known Jesse personally, and Charley would sit in rapt attention as the ancient would reminisce about some long-ago outlaw escapade that may have happened only in his imagination.

Charley didn't care. His own imagination was fueled by the bank robber whom he envisioned as a sort of Robin Hood, giving back to the common folk what the banks often took by intimidation, if not sheer force.

As Charley got older, he spent less time reading and more hours in the bars of nearby towns. Evenings and weekends found Charley drinking a brew called Chocktaw Beer, an ale he so favored that his drinking buddies adopted the name to refer to him.

At the age of 16, Choc saw the futility in trying to make a living from the land and, perhaps inspired by his outlaw heroes, decided to head west. With little money, Choc was forced to adopt a hobo lifestyle, hopping freight trains and grabbing whatever other forms of transportation he could find along the way.

His strong physique never left him at a loss for meal money, although the work mostly consisted of those same sod-turning chores he'd hoped to escape: hard, blistering work for little pay. These disappointing stopovers only intensified Choc's desire to create his own path in life, which he was determined to accomplish by using his own special talents.

Choc's ambitions finally found an opportunity in Wichita, through a chance association with a white-haired, pipe-smoking Irishman named John Callahan. Callahan worked primarily as a "fence," but with Fagin-like appeal he offered himself as a mentor to any serious would-be criminal. The highly impressionable Choc immediately came under the influence of the charismatic Irishman.

Callahan nurtured a spirit of larceny in his charges. He taught them how to become effective thieves. Although Choc had limited schooling and had shown little interest in classroom studies, he became an honor student in the practical education supplied by Callahan. Mostly Choc ran errands for Callahan, and it was through Choc's frequent contacts with the Irishman's outlaw and ex-con cronies that he further developed a yearning for fast living and easy money.

But Choc's strong fundamental upbringing wielded its own influence, and in 1924 he decided to go back home to Oklahoma and try honest work one last time. But soil and climate conditions had grown worse, and Choc quickly became even more frustrated at farming than he was before he'd left. The bright spot in his dreary existence was his courtship of 16-year-old Ruby Hardgraves. When Ruby announced to Floyd that she was three months pregnant with his child, Choc, ever the gentleman, married her on June 28.

Four days after Christmas, Ruby presented Choc with a son, Charles Dempsey Floyd, known thereafter by his middle name, given because of Choc's admiration for boxer Jack Dempsey.

Choc was immensely proud of Dempsey and showed him off at every opportunity. But even the love for his son could not curb Choc's increasingly restless nature. Choc was mostly discouraged by his inability to provide a decent living for Ruby and Dempsey. He saw his efforts mirroring the frustrations experienced by his father, and in 1925, he was determined to make a change.

As Ruby explained it, "At first Charley was a hardworking farmer. But we never hardly saw any money, while the neighbor boys always seemed to have plenty."

Charley went off to work, he said, in the harvest fields. Suddenly, Ruby began receiving large sums of money, which she knew her husband could not have earned by honest means.

The truth was that Choc had traded five gallons of moonshine for a pearl-handled .44. With some friends he rode the rails to St. Louis, where on September 11, 1925, they robbed couriers of a $12,000 payroll bound for the Kroger Grocery and Bakery Company.

But the robbers left themselves open to identification, and when Choc began flaunting his "windfall" back home in Sallisaw, he and accomplice Fred Hildebrand were promptly arrested, shackled and transported back to St. Louis.

Charles Arthur Floyd (Prisoner #29078) began a five-year stretch at the Missouri State Penitentiary in Jefferson City.

"Doing hard time on a nickel" was how Choc described it.

Like John Dillinger, Choc entered prison as a criminal novice, but during his sentence, he ingratiated himself with the big leaguers from whom he picked up valuable tips in criminal procedure.

Choc was paroled on March 7, 1929. Just prior to his release, he learned that Ruby had filed for divorce. Although Choc did not contest it and would remain close to Ruby and Dempsey, he was embittered by this consequence of his imprisonment and decided that, from then on, he would play by his own rules. He also swore that he would never again see the inside of a prison.

Yet, within months of his release from Jeff City, Choc was jailed on three separate occasions: twice on suspicion of robbery and once on a vagrancy charge. His entry into a life of full-time crime was hardly auspicious.

But two events would forever change Choc Floyd's image and his reputation. The story goes that while Choc was visiting a brothel in Kansas City, Missouri, the madam, Sadie "Mother" Ash took an immediate liking to him and purred, "I want you for myself, pretty boy." The moniker stuck, even though Floyd, like "Baby Face" Nelson, detested it and would never allow it to be used in his presence.

The second incident was far more serious. His father Walter had been shot to death over a dispute with a man named Jim Mills. Choc returned home from Kansas City for both his father's burial and Jim Mills' trial. Because Walter had been the aggressor in their fatal confrontation, Mills was acquitted. But shortly thereafter, Jim Mills vanished, never to be seen again.

A local resident summed up the prevailing attitude when he merely shrugged and said, "Choc done what he had to."

Charles Arthur "Pretty Boy" Floyd, public enemy and hillbilly folk hero

Okies had their own way of dispensing justice, and it was evident to all that Choc Floyd had gone "a-huntin'." Still, the law was looking for Choc, so he hightailed it back to Kansas City ("Tom's Town," as it was then called because it operated under the corrupt influence of Thomas Pendergast). In 1929, Kansas City was a place where wanted criminals could move about freely, and it was where Pretty Boy Floyd hoped to make his reputation.

He worked as a freelance bootlegger and made himself known to the city's most notorious underworld characters, who advanced his career by sharing their knowledge in everything from effective bank-robbery techniques to how to handle a machine gun.

Choc teamed up with fellow Jefferson City ex-cons James Bradley and Bob Amos, along with a seasoned Toledo tough named Jack Atkins, and the four retreated to a small cottage in Akron, Ohio, to plot a succession of bank heists.

They hit their first bank on Wednesday, February 5, 1930—The Farmers and Merchant Bank in Sylvania, Ohio. Choc and his accomplices rushed into the bank and lined the customers up against the wall. Almost immediately, they ran into trouble. The cashier was unable to open the vault because it was time locked for another five hours.

Choc was furious and snapped back the hammer on his revolver. "I'll give you just two minutes to open the safe."

When the cashier protested that it couldn't be done, Choc pistol-whipped the unfortunate man. Then, a gas station employee across the street noticed the commotion and called the fire department, who chased the fleeing outlaws in a fire truck. Choc and his crew got away, but their efforts netted them only $2000.

Unfortunately, James Bradley and Bob Amos didn't stay free for long. On the night of March 8, they were leaving a birthday celebration in Akron when police spotted them. The pair tried to get away by car, but they were inebriated and crashed into another vehicle.

As police moved in to arrest them, Bradley pulled out his pistol and shot Patrolman Harland F. Manes point-blank in the stomach, mortally wounding him. The other officers opened fire, but Bradley managed to stumble free into the darkness. Amos wasn't so lucky. He was quickly apprehended before he could extricate himself from the wreckage.

Akron police quickly intensified their search for the cop killer. The following day, acting on a tip, they burst into the gang's hideout and arrested both Bradley and Pretty Boy Floyd, giving both men a brutal beating.

Bradley was sentenced to die in the electric chair. (Moments before walking the green mile, Bradley reportedly joked to the padre: "I'm due for a shocking this evening.") Amos received a life sentence, and Choc, although acquitted on the murder charge, was given 12 to 15 years for his participation in the Sylvania bank job.

"I'll never be taken alive," Choc had bragged to his fellow inmates prior to sentencing. "I'd rather be killed than serve a year in prison."

Choc took his vow seriously, and on Wednesday, December 10, 1930, en route to the Ohio State Penitentiary, he kicked out a window and hurled himself from the speeding train. He quickly got to his feet and broke into a run. By the time the train could grind to a halt, Choc had a good half-mile on his pursuers.

Although Choc was free, he was a wanted man and would always be on the run. Hitchhiking along back roads, he traveled at night through small Midwestern towns in his journey to Kansas City, the one place where he knew he'd be safe.

Choc lay low for a while before teaming with Willis "Billy the Killer" Miller. Although younger than Floyd's previous partners, Miller was no lightweight. He'd earned his deadly reputation when he gunned down his own brother in a duel over a woman.

Choc and Miller began their criminal partnership by robbing rural filling stations. Then, throughout the spring of 1931, they graduated to bank heists in Arkansas, Kentucky and northern Wisconsin.

While cooling their heels in Kansas City, they were boarders at Mother Ash's whorehouse, where other comforts besides food and lodging were provided. The two had fallen for Mother Ash's daughters-in-law, Rose Ash and Beulah Baird. A short time later the bodies of Rose and Beulah's husbands were found in a ditch across the state line. Naturally, Choc and Miller were prime suspects in the homicides—they had actually already taken up with the widows. However, it is more likely that Wallace and Walter Ash, both killed execution-style, had paid the ultimate penalty for their own criminal activities.* At any rate, Choc Floyd and "Billy the Killer" Miller were hot. Traveling back into Arkansas and Kentucky with their new female companions, they knocked over Depression banks throughout the two states for cash rewards that never exceeded $4000.

On the afternoon of April 16, police in Bowling Green, Ohio (who had been watching the suspicious quartet since their arrival in town several days before), contacted Chief Carl "Shorty" Galliher and Officer Ralph Castner with their concerns that the four were frequently spotted in the vicinity of a bank on South Main Street.

The two police officers hurried to the location where they noticed three strangers—a man and two women, loitering around the bank. They failed to note the heavyset man standing across the street, but Choc certainly saw them as they emerged from the squad car.

"Bill, duck!" he shouted.

Miller whipped out his .45 but only managed to get one shot off before he was hit in the gut, and his lifeless body toppled onto the sidewalk.

Choc, legs widespread, desperado-style, drew his own pistols and opened fire. The two girls screamed and ran for cover, but Beulah fell when a stray bullet penetrated her skull. Officer

---

*The two brothers were low-level underworld characters involved in narcotics and prostitution, and they worked as runners for the city's north-end combine.

Castner was hit twice, and although seriously injured with a slug in his abdomen, continued to exchange gunfire with Floyd.

Finally, with his ammunition exhausted, Choc darted down an alleyway, trying to get to where their car was parked. Galliher took off in pursuit, but Choc sprinted with a speed that belied his size. Before the lawman could catch up, Floyd's auto was already spewing exhaust.

The story of the bloody Bowling Green shootout made national headlines, and Charley Floyd's reputation was sealed when Madam Ash anxiously asked reporters: "Did they get Pretty Boy?" Overnight, the name Pretty Boy Floyd became a household name.

Officer Castner died from his abdominal wound the following day. He was only 28. A charge of first-degree murder was leveled against Floyd along with a $1000 reward offered for his capture.

But County Sheriff Bruce C. Pratt first warned, "Extreme caution must be used when approaching Floyd, as he will not hesitate to shoot."

Choc felt like a porker on a spit, getting hotter each time he turned. He returned to Kansas City where he kept a low profile, while tending to his former bootlegging trade. Much of the money he made from his low-income enterprise he sent to girlfriend Beulah Baird, who was convalescing from her head wound.

Trouble just seemed to follow Choc. His next streak of notoriety occurred on the evening of July 20, when Prohibition agents broke into the room he was renting above a flower-shop-cum-bootlegging establishment. He'd been sitting at a table playing cards with nine other criminal types and, feigning drunkenness, slowly rose to his feet.

One agent noticed him. "Hey!" he shouted to the others. "It's Pretty Boy Floyd."

Choc immediately assumed his deadly wide-legged stance, brandishing two automatics that seemed to appear out of nowhere. Special Agent Curtis C. Burks had the misfortune of being the first to step into Choc's lethal fusillade and had most of his head blown from his body. Four other men were wounded in the quick exchange of gunfire. Floyd's current companion, 23-year-old Joe Careo was blown apart by a shotgun blast. Choc himself managed to get away in the customary "hail of bullets."

Counting himself lucky at his second narrow escape, Choc decided to return to the Oklahoma hills, where he knew he would find acceptance and protection among his own people. While slowly making his way back home, Choc was often forced to resort to living off the land, and the hardship helped him rediscover his passion for the simple country life he had chosen to abandon. He could barely contain his excitement at his long-anticipated reunion with Ruby and six-year-old son Dempsey.

Choc and Ruby discovered that they were still in love with each other. Although Ruby had since remarried, she didn't hesitate to pack up Dempsey and their belongings and drive away with Choc.

Choc was the happiest and most contented he'd been in a long while. To all appearances, the Floyds resumed a happy family life, but Choc couldn't seem to tame his criminal tendencies. Teaming up with 40-year-old preacher-turned-thief George Birdwell, Choc embarked on a bank-robbing spree unparalleled in the Southwest.

Armed with his machine gun, the immaculately dressed Pretty Boy Floyd would stroll into a bank in broad daylight and then chat politely with employees while they filled up his satchel with cash. With times being so tough, their personal take from each score barely totaled in the hundreds of dollars. But Choc and Birdwell received added satisfaction by breaking into strongboxes to tear up any first mortgage deeds they could find, then leaving in their wake scattered bills of all denominations for hungry and homeless citizens.

Choc was often recognized as he and Birdwell knocked off small-town banks throughout Oklahoma. Town folk would pleasantly greet the gangster and then let him go on about his business.

On December 12, 1931, Choc pulled off two bank heists—one in Paden and another in Castle, Oklahoma. On April 9, 1932, a bold Oklahoma lawman named Erv Kelley who had been trailing Floyd for three months tried to ambush Pretty Boy near Bixby. A machine-gun battle ensued, and when the smoke cleared, it was Kelley who lay dead. Yet, despite the severity of his crimes, Choc remained revered and protected by his fellow Oklahomans.

One day, Choc even had the audacity to walk into his hometown bank in Sallisaw. Several citizens casually watched the familiar figure stroll towards the Sallisaw bank with a machine gun under his arm.

"Howdy, Choc," one of the men greeted. "Where're yuh headed?"

"Howdy, Newt," Choc replied. "Goin' to rob the bank," he added, as nonchalantly as if he were going for a haircut.

"Give 'em hell, Choc!" shouted another farmer.

Choc relieved the bank of $2530, after which he told teller Bob Riggs that he would have to come along as a hostage, to which Riggs readily agreed. As Choc drove away, throwing out handfuls of bills, he was cheered on by people approving of his defiance of a system that had robbed so many of them of their homes and livelihoods. A reporter later described the event as "the hometown performance of a great actor who has made it good on Broadway."

On another occasion, when Floyd was on the run and was homesick to see his mother, he wrote to the Sallisaw sheriff:

"I'm coming to see my mother. If you're smart you won't try to stop me." According to the story, the sheriff obliged.

Choc and Birdwell moved on to Henryetta, Oklahoma, where they hit the jackpot with a take amounting to $11,352. Choc was robbing so many banks and money-lending companies that his "good intentions" backfired when insurance companies began doubling their rates in Oklahoma. The governor of the state took advantage of the situation to reverse public sympathies towards Floyd. He offered a $6000 reward for "Choc" Floyd—dead or alive.

Choc declared, "I have robbed no one but moneyed men."

Unfortunately, no matter how much his neighbors applauded his Robin Hood banditry, money spoke louder, and Choc knew that he would have to watch his back.

Adding to his troubles was that George Birdwell had begun drinking, and as he was not a man to handle his liquor, Choc was forced to part company with him. (Police killed Birdwell soon afterwards when he attempted to go it alone on a bank robbery in Boley, Oklahoma.)

In the meantime, *Startling Detective* magazine featured a cover story on Pretty Boy Floyd and sweetened the reward pot by offering their own $4000 bounty.

Choc was an expert at navigating the backwoods trails of the Cookson Hills and could always stay ahead of the law. Many hill folk still sheltered him, and Choc always paid handsomely for their protection and hospitality. But Choc Floyd, again separated from his wife and son, was tiring of life on the run.

In early 1933, Choc was implicated in the killing of two police officers near Columbus, Missouri. The authorities intensified the manhunt and upped the demand for Floyd's capture, or preferably, his death. Even though he was innocent, the resulting publicity made him responsible for far more crimes than he'd ever committed.

In April, Choc took on another partner, Adam "Eddie" Richetti. Figuring there was no turning back, Choc led Richetti on a reckless run of bank jobs throughout Oklahoma, Missouri and Arkansas.

And then on the morning of June 17, 1933, seven local and federal officers escorting Oklahoma bandit Frank "Jelly" Nash to Leavenworth Penitentiary were ambushed outside Union Station in Kansas City. It was a bloodbath. Five men, including Nash, were slaughtered in what was believed to be an attempt to free the bandit from his federal captors. The main triggerman was a heavyset individual whom witnesses were prodded into identifying as Pretty Boy Floyd.

Floyd, then the nation's most wanted bad man, had the misfortune of being in Kansas City at the time. Further witnesses, such as Blackie Audett, later claimed that the real gunmen were a Syndicate crew that definitely did not include Floyd.

In his 1954 book *Rap Sheet*, Audett writes that the FBI had to solve the case quickly since one of their own had been killed and so pinned it on Pretty Boy, who was already expendable in their eyes. Choc tried to defend himself against the heinous charge, going so far as to write a letter to the Kansas City Police, which read:

> *Dear Sirs:*
> *I, Charles Floyd, want it made known that I did not participate in the massacre of officers at Kansas City.*
> *Charles Floyd*

In the aftermath of the Kansas City Massacre, Floyd's situation became so desperate that he even offered to surrender himself voluntarily, provided he not be tried on murder charges. The offer was refused. By this time, Floyd could see no reprieve in his future and no reason for him to continue proclaiming his innocence in the Kansas City Massacre unless, of course, he truly was not guilty of the crime.

In a 1995 interview, Floyd's son Dempsey spoke in his father's defense: "My father wasn't a hired killer. He robbed banks and got all the money he needed. Why would he take a fee for killing police who were trying to transfer another criminal?"

Beyond Dempsey's contention that Floyd would not have worked as a killer-for-hire, another point to consider is the unlikelihood of the wanted Pretty Boy Floyd jeopardizing his safety in Kansas City by participating in the daylight shooting of federal officers. Unfortunately, Floyd's protests fell on deaf ears. The nation was so outraged by the slayings that they were easily prejudiced by the resulting press and judged Floyd guilty (especially when further reminded that the gangster had killed his share of policemen during his bank robbery sprees). To make matters worse, his partner Eddie Richetti was also identified as one of the gunmen.

Choc reckoned that the only place they might be safe was back in the Cookson Hills. There remained a local bounty on his head, but Choc knew that enough good folk in the county would offer them shelter and perhaps a hot meal.

Choc's knowledge of the region helped to keep both him and Richetti out of sight even as a contingent of federal agents, military officers, local police, sheriffs and National Guardsmen descended on Oklahoma and fanned out on the tricky terrain of the Cookson Hills. But Choc knew that they couldn't isolate themselves forever and suggested to his partner that they leave Oklahoma and try their luck out East. Just because there was a price on his head didn't mean that Choc was going to quit robbing banks.

As he explained to Richetti, "They're gonna get me, ain't much doubt of that. So we might as well keep doin' what we been doin.'"

After spending some time in Buffalo, Choc and Richetti drove into Ohio. An accident with their car forced the two to continue on foot, where their appearance prompted a phone call from a suspicious local farmer to Police Chief John H. Fultz of Wellsville.

Fultz and two deputized citizens drove out to the location where the pair had been spotted. Choc got the drop on Fultz, but in a moment of confusion, the police chief managed to draw his .32 revolver and exchange fire with the two. Floyd repeatedly pumped the trigger of his handgun, and he managed to get away yet again. Richetti wasn't so lucky.

When FBI chief J. Edgar Hoover learned that it was Adam Richetti who had been captured, he immediately dispatched his ace, Special Agent Melvin Purvis, to question him concerning the whereabouts of Pretty Boy Floyd.

By now the era of the Depression Day Desperado was in its twilight. Bonnie and Clyde were dead, so (presumably) was John Dillinger. The remaining public enemies and lesser bad men were feeling the squeeze, many having only weeks to live. And within just a few months, the only bandit still at large would be Alvin "Old Creepy" Karpis.

Years later, Karpis remembered a disheveled Choc and Richetti meeting with him in a parking lot shortly after the Kansas City Massacre and proposing a team-up, which Karpis promptly declined.

"I wished them well, but there wasn't an outlaw gang alive who wanted anything to do with Pretty Boy Floyd," Karpis recalled.

Meanwhile, Melvin Purvis flew into Wellsville and interrogated Richetti. In addition, he and the dozen agents assigned to him conducted raids on known Richetti hangouts and posted guards at the bridge across the Ohio River.

Purvis was frustrated by the numerous unconfirmed sightings of Pretty Boy Floyd that flooded into his office. It seemed as if every impoverished farmer throughout the Midwest gambled on hitting the jackpot by giving information on the outlaw's whereabouts. But the truth was, no one knew where Floyd was hiding.

On October 22, Choc, unwashed and unshaven, appeared on the doorstep of Ellen Conkle's farmhouse.

"I apologize for the way I look," Choc said to her. "But I'm lost and hungry and wonder if I might get something to eat. I'll gladly pay you."

Choc explained to Mrs. Conkle that he'd gotten drunk the night before and wandered off from his brother during a squirrel-hunting trip.

The woman invited Choc inside, and he took a seat at the kitchen table. She fed him a fine meal of spareribs, potatoes and, for dessert, pumpkin pie. He insisted on paying her at least a dollar for her hospitality.

Floyd had noticed a Model A Ford in the yard. After dinner, he asked Mrs. Conkle's brother, Stewart Dyke, if he would give him a lift. Dyke offered to drive him as far as Clarkson. As Floyd climbed into the backseat, Stewart got behind the wheel and struggled to turn over the engine. At that point, two cars drove in procession down the main road. The fading autumn sunlight glinted off their polished exteriors, a telltale sign that these freshly cleaned vehicles were not common to this route.

Purvis and his men just happened to be driving by the Conkle farm while they were scouting the vicinity for Floyd. When Choc saw that the two cars were heavily manned, he panicked, drew his gun and made a mad dash across an open pasture.

The lawmen spotted the fleeing figure and pulled onto the Conkle property. They leaped from their cars and took up various positions around the farmhouse. Choc had already sprinted about 50 feet into the field.

"Floyd, halt!" Purvis ordered, but Choc kept running, zigzagging, trying to make the crest of a distant hill and the shelter of its trees.

Purvis gave the order: "Fire!"

The peaceful country twilight quiet was momentarily shattered as a single volley of gunfire brought down Pretty Boy Floyd. The agents rushed to the fallen man and carried him to the shade of an apple tree.

"Why didn't you halt when I yelled?" Purvis gently asked.

The dying Choc replied, "If I'd gotten in them woods, you'd never have got me."

He then told the agents to take the .45 automatic tucked inside his trousers. "I have no more use for it," he said.

Purvis questioned Choc about the Kansas City Massacre.

Choc's eyes flashed wide. "I didn't do it! Had no part in it!" he responded with a choking breath.

Purvis leaned in close. "You are Pretty Boy Floyd?"

"I'm Charles Arthur Floyd," were the last words the outlaw spoke.

On his person, the agents found $120 in cash and a watch with 10 notches carved into the rim, legend has it, one for each man he had killed.

His people buried him in the Cookson Hills. Reportedly, more than 40,000 people from over 20 states filed past his body at his funeral. It was a far grander sendoff than that accorded his partner Adam "Eddie" Richetti, who was put to death in the gas chamber at Jefferson City on October 7, 1938. His body was sent to his brother for burial.

The official file on Pretty Boy Floyd was closed, but four decades after his death a new controversy came to light. In 1979, a retired police captain named Chester Smith who was present at the shooting came forward to publicly declare that the outlaw's killing did not occur exactly as reported. He stated that Pretty Boy Floyd was assassinated.

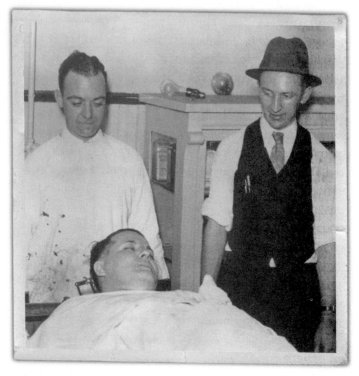

The body of Pretty Boy Floyd lies on a slab in an Ohio mortuary after his killing or "assassination." Photographs of deceased gangsters were profitable for news services during the heyday of the public enemy. Many famous blood-soaked images of criminals at the scenes of their deaths were published. Also a popular subject for photographers were pictures of their subjects either stretched out in the morgue or in funereal repose. A crime photographer of the time later commented that these pictures were important to public morale because they showed that the law was ridding society of criminals. By graphically displaying portraits of corpses, people could see the human element missing from newspaper headlines that previously touted the invincibility of the gangster.

According to Smith, Pretty Boy was merely wounded in the shooting, but when he refused to answer Purvis' questions about his involvement in the Kansas City Massacre, the agent ordered Agent Herman Hollis to "execute" Floyd.

When Purvis was asked by the aghast witness why he had ordered Floyd shot, the agent replied: "Mr. Hoover, my boss, told me to bring him in dead."

However, W.E. "Bud" Hopton, one of the four FBI agents at the Conkle farm, disputed Smith's account, maintaining that the bullets that killed Floyd were those fired into him as he fled across the field. He added that Agent Hollis (killed only a month later in the final shootout with Baby Face Nelson) wasn't even present during the manhunt.

The official FBI report leaves no doubt either to Pretty Boy Floyd's participation in the Kansas City Massacre or the events surrounding his death. But as with the debate concerning John Dillinger's true demise, witness testimony and investigative probing into the facts have prompted some to question the validity of official records regarding Charles Arthur "Pretty Boy" Floyd, and at the very least, have added a shading of gray into areas previously accepted as purely black or white.

Let Ma Joad have the last word:

> *But the folks that knowed him didn't hurt 'im. He wasn't mad at them. Finally, they run 'im down and killed 'im. No matter how they say it in the paper how he was bad, that's how it was.*

CHAPTER FIVE

Ma Barker and Her Boys:

Ma (1872–1935), Herman (1894–1927),
Lloyd (1896–1949), Arthur "Doc" (1899–1939),
Fred (1902–1935)

"Ma Barker and her sons…constituted the
toughest gang of hoodlums the FBI has ever
been called upon to eliminate."

–J. Edgar Hoover

WHETHER OR NOT SHE WAS TRULY THE MASTERMIND behind
the Barker-Karpis Gang whose Depression-era crime spree
included everything from bank robbery to kidnapping to
murder, there is no question that Kate "Ma" Barker was the
matriarch of the most bloodthirsty band of brothers ever to
commit carnage across the Midwest.

Short (5'2"), stout, unassuming Kate Barker nearly single-
parented her four sons in conditions of appalling poverty.
Their father, George, had no real influence on his sons' development because each of the boys—Herman, Arthur ("Doc"),
Lloyd and Fred—was "Ma's boy." And each possessed a vicious
killer instinct, perhaps the result of a genetic imbalance or
maybe the sociological impact of their hungry upbringing
and parental permissiveness. Or were the boys psychologi-
cally warped by an unhealthy and perhaps incestuous devotion to their mother fostered by Ma herself?

"Notorious" Kate "Ma" Barker, of whom no official police photographs exist

Alvin Karpis, the "adopted" son of Ma Barker, admitted that the old woman could be controlling, especially when it came to her sons' lady friends. Ma wanted to be the central woman in their lives, and understandably this often created friction with boys who already had a rebellious nature.

Freddie Barker, Karpis' best friend and the most wild and undisciplined of the bunch, complained incessantly about Ma's domineering ways. Yet his love for her never wavered, and when the lengthy FBI siege on their hideout in Florida ended and those famous posthumous photographs were taken, it was Ma and her youngest son who lay side by side in the morgue.

J. Edgar Hoover, although devoted to his own mother, never had a kind word for Kate Barker. After Ma's eldest son, Herman, died by his own hand, Hoover remarked that it was his suicide that transformed Ma Barker "from an animal mother of the she-wolf type to a veritable beast of prey."

Alvin Karpis (who never had a kind word for Hoover) was both amused and frequently outraged at the Bureau's claim that this old hillbilly woman was the "brains" behind the gang, which, during their four-year run, was unquestionably one of the most successful outlaw bands of the era, accumulating at least $3 million with their various criminal endeavors.

"It's no insult to Ma's memory that she just didn't have the intelligence or know-how to direct us on a robbery," said Karpis in his memoirs. "It wouldn't have occurred to her to get involved in our business, and we always made a point of only discussing our scores when Ma wasn't around. We'd either leave her at home or we'd send her to a movie. Ma saw a lot of movies."

He added that Ma was a homebody who enjoyed simple pleasures, such as working on jigsaw puzzles and listening to hillbilly music on the radio.

Harvey Bailey, a veteran bank robber who occasionally worked with the Barker-Karpis Gang, summed it up even more succinctly: "The old woman couldn't even organize breakfast."

It was an image far removed from the hard-as-nails, gun-toting public enemy depicted in popular culture. Yet this image of Ma Barker became so firmly entrenched in the public consciousness that just five years after her death she received on-screen immortality when actress Blanche Yurka portrayed "Ma Webster" in *Queen of the Mob*, a *Persons in Hiding* "B" picture produced by Paramount Studios. Not even hardcore cases like Dillinger, Nelson or Floyd had as yet been accorded cinematic posterity.

While it is probably too late to rewrite history, the claims of Alvin Karpis and others regarding Ma's participation in the gang deserve renewed consideration. If Ma Barker truly was the feared criminal of legend, why does not one official police photograph of her exist? Why was not one set of fingertips taken while she was alive? This is strong evidence since every other public enemy of the time, including Ma's sons, had mug shots taken and fingerprints on record.

Karpis further pointed out that no one had even heard of "Ma" Barker until after "she was slaughtered by the FBI," and it was only then that this "ridiculous" legend came to light.

"She certainly knew we were criminals," Karpis said. "But her participation in our careers was limited to one function. When we traveled together, we moved as a mother and her sons. What could look more innocent?"

Innocent indeed.

The story behind Ma Barker and her killer brood had the same grassroots beginnings as so many others destined for Depression Day notoriety.

Arizona Donnie Clark entered the world on an unrecorded date in 1872. She grew up 18 miles northwest of Springfield, Missouri, the same region that spawned Frank and Jesse James. As a young girl, Arizona Kate (called Arrie) worshipped and even fantasized about Jesse, whom she had once seen ride through Carthage with the equally famous Younger brothers at his side. Kate was devastated at age 10, when she learned of Jesse's death and abhorred the fact that he was shot in the back by the cowardly traitor Bob Ford. (Ironically, her own boy Freddie had no qualms about shooting victims from behind if the situation warranted it.)

As a young woman, Kate was considered quite attractive, and men throughout the county were eager to court her. But her upbringing in the Ozark Mountains had toughened her, and potential suitors learned fast that Kate Clark was no pushover, although she did indulge in quainter pastimes, including playing the fiddle and reading her bible. She was a devout churchgoer who also enjoyed singing in the choir.

In 1892, 20-year-old Kate married a sharecropper named George Barker, and the two moved to Aurora, Missouri, where over the next several years all four of their sons were born: Herman in 1894, Lloyd in 1896, Arthur in 1899 and Fred in 1902.

Like their mother, all the boys were short of stature. Herman was the tallest at 5'5". Both he and Arthur were of a stockier build, while Lloyd and Fred were slender. Their unimposing physiques and plain, farm-boy features were deceiving and gave no hint of the murderous souls lurking within.

As Alvin Karpis later recalled, "Freddie was a natural killer. And while Doc didn't look dangerous, he was a lethal operator."

When Herman and Lloyd reached school age, the family moved to Webb City, Missouri, a mining community, where George sought more lucrative employment in vain.

George was an easygoing man, but completely deficient in his parental responsibilities, deferring to his wife in every decision regarding the boys' upbringing. When the boys began getting into trouble more frequently and he tried halfheartedly to assert discipline, Kate angrily reprimanded him. She dismissed their fighting, vandalism and petty thievery as "mischievous pranks" and then fed them a good dinner. Kate Barker defended her boys even more vehemently against neighbors who often came to her door to demand that she do something about her boys' delinquency.

George became so deflated by his role in the family that when personally confronted by his neighbors, he merely shrugged his shoulders and said, "Go talk with Mother. She handles the boys."

When even the congregation at her beloved church began criticizing the actions of the Barker boys, Kate immediately stopped attending Sunday services, fervently regarding her fellow parishioners as judgmental and unchristian.

"If the good people of this town don't take a likin' to my boys," she said with self-righteous indignation, "then these so-called good people know what they can do!"

But the "boyhood pranks" of the Barker brothers began taking on more serious criminal overtones as each entered puberty. As the oldest, Herman naturally set the standard for the others. He was a sadistic sociopath with complete disregard for law and order, people or property.

In 1910, at age 16, Herman along with brother Lloyd established an adolescent gang of burglars and roughnecks who became known as the Central Park Gang. That same year Herman was arrested for petty thievery. But before the police could file charges, Ma stormed into the station and caused such a ruckus that the officers on duty finally just slapped Herman with a warning before releasing him into his mother's custody.

Ma's younger sons were already well on their way to following in Herman's footsteps. Ma still stood behind her boys, but the persistent demands from the citizenry that she take a more stern approach to their antisocial behavior was becoming a plain nuisance. Finally, in 1915, after Herman was arrested again for robbery (and released again into his mother's custody after she went before the authorities and tearfully pleaded for leniency), Ma decided to move her boys to Tulsa, Oklahoma.

"My boys are marked," she said bitterly. "They won't ever be leavin' them alone."

Perhaps Ma hoped a new environment might curb her sons' wild tendencies. But each boy was by now an ingrained criminal, and each time one of them was brought before the law, it was Ma who came running to their defense, inevitably getting them freed using her own persuasive techniques.

By 1915, the boys began making the acquaintance of some big-name underworld characters, many of whom were fugitives from the law. At Freddie's urging, Ma opened her Tulsa house as a hideout for such notorious bank robbers as Al Spencer and Frank "Jelly" Nash. Ma never complained, and she welcomed each of her boys' new friends as part of the family.

Herman, Doc, Freddie and Lloyd received much of their education in crime merely by listening to these professionals map out their bank-robbery strategies at the kitchen table. The promise of a life far more exciting and rewarding than their own small-potatoes thievery inevitably lit a fire under each of the boys. As the oldest, Herman was the first to strike out on his own.

Ma was distressed; his brothers were impressed. George, knowing that whatever he said made no impression on his eldest son, would have told his boy to do what he felt he had to do.

Herman drove off with Ray Terrill, one of Ma's "boarders," and became a member of the Kimes-Terrill gang, who knocked over banks throughout Texas, Oklahoma and Missouri during the early 1920s.

Lloyd was the next Barker to grow restless. In 1922 he tried to hold up a post office, but was quickly apprehended. Since his crime was a federal offense, Lloyd Barker was sentenced to a maximum term of 25 years in Leavenworth Penitentiary.

That same year, Doc Barker achieved the most notoriety of the brothers when he was sent to the Oklahoma State

Penitentiary at McAlester for life. Doc had committed his first adult crime in 1918 when he stole a government car. He was captured and sent to prison, where he began a pattern of escapes and recaptures that would eventually lead him into Alcatraz.

However, in 1922, Doc was the first of the Barkers to be indicted for murder, charged with killing a night watchman at the St. John's Hospital in Tulsa while trying to steal a drug shipment. Doc always swore he was innocent (his protests steadfastly supported by Ma), and although he spent 13 years behind bars, he was eventually exonerated when a California thief came forward and confessed to the crime.

Ma had only her youngest, Freddie, still at home. His boyhood "mischievousness" included robbery and vagrancy, and he spent time in a reformatory. He was ready to join his brothers and embark on his own criminal destiny. In 1926, he tried to rob the bank in Windfield, Kansas. As he was making his getaway, a townsman laid him cold with a well-aimed brick to the head. For his efforts, Freddie was handed a 5-to-10-year jail term in the Kansas State Penitentiary at Lansing. Before beginning his sentence, Freddie jumped a $10,000 bail bond put up by his mother. But Freddie wasn't as intent on escape as he was in raising the cash with more robberies to pay back his debt to Ma.

Herman was the only Barker brother still free, but his luck was running out. He and partner Ray Terrill were finally apprehended while robbing a Missouri bank. They managed to escape before reaching the jailhouse and sped off in a stolen automobile.

"We won't get far; we're short of funds," Herman grumbled, as he pushed the car to its limit. The pair needed some quick traveling money.

They drove into Newton, Kansas, where they held up an icehouse. As expected, their take was meager, but at least it would see them out of town. Farther up the road, police flagged them down at a roadblock. Ray Terrill urged Herman to run the blockade, but his partner instead slowed to a stop.

"You crazy, Barker?" Terrill demanded to know. "You want us to get caught?"

Herman just smiled a slow, chilling smile.

Officer J.E. Marshall approached the vehicle. "Could I see some identification?" he asked, leaning inside the open window of the car.

Herman responded by grabbing Marshall around the neck and firing a Luger into his head. Herman then slammed the car into gear, but Marshall's partner, who was standing on the opposite side of the car, quickly opened fire, sending so many bullets into Herman that Barker turned the Luger on himself to finish the job.

When Ma heard the news, she refused to believe that her eldest son had committed suicide and instead saw Herman's death as a police execution.

"A Barker don't do things like that," she said adamantly.

Ma was alone and lonely. Herman was dead, her other three boys were in jail, and she had left her husband George by this time. She was determined to expedite the release of her boys, and she raised the needed capital to pay for good lawyers by once again providing a "safe house" for fugitives from the law.

But Freddie wasn't complaining. The Barker reputation served him well in prison, and he soon became acquainted with a dour-faced younger convict who would become his closest friend and confederate in crime—Alvin Karpis.

Years later Karpis would fondly remember his first meeting with Freddie Barker: "It was an unforgettable event, not because it was all that dramatic, but just because it was so pleasant."

When the grinning, gold-toothed Freddie introduced himself to Karpis en route to the mess hall, an instant friendship

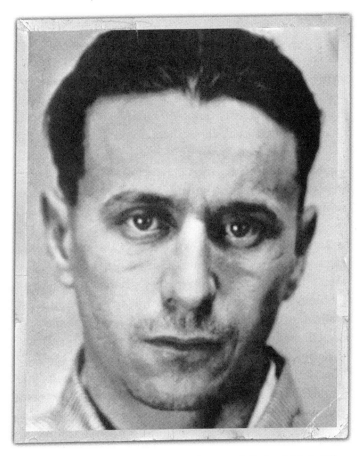

Freddie Barker, the last born and most lethal of Ma's killer brood

was forged. They ate dinner together, then later got high on marijuana in the prison yard.

Freddie arranged for Karpis to be transferred to his cell where he proved to be a gracious host, sharing many of his comforts and food delicacies, such as canned chicken, fresh bread, pies and pastries.

Karpis learned a lot from Freddie Barker, who was six years his senior, and they planned to team up after their release. Because of Kate Barker's efforts, Freddie finally walked away from Lansing on March 20, 1931. Karpis was released soon afterwards, and he met "Ma" for the first time when Freddie told him that he could get his address from her.

The memory of their meeting also remained clear to Karpis, further prompting him to scoff at the FBI's presentation of Kate Barker as a murderous, calculating gang leader. He remembered walking up to a dilapidated old house where a dumpy old woman in a pair of bib overalls over a man's sweater was trying to nail a window screen into its frame.

Karpis and Ma got along well, and it wasn't long before Ma began regarding Alvin as one of her boys. Ma had taken up with a man named Arthur V. Dunlop, but it was clear to Karpis that her true devotion was to her sons. He often saw Ma's temper flare when it came to their lady friends. She simply did not want any female competition, and this extended to Karpis' girls as well.

Freddie and Karpis partnered on some minor burglaries in and around Missouri, Kansas and other Midwest states before Freddie was picked up on an earlier charge and jailed in Claremont, Oklahoma. Freddie escaped and hooked up with Karpis in Tulsa. Although he had the gaunt, pale look of a man on the lam, Freddie was eager to get back to work.

He proposed a bank robbery in Mountain View, Missouri. Together with a couple of other ex-cons, Bill Weaver and Jimmie Wilson, they broke into the bank at 3:00 AM and merely waited for the employees to arrive for work at 9:00 AM. They forced the bank workers to open the vault, and after scooping up all the money, forced the employees inside the metal enclosure before driving off in Freddie's car. To discourage pursuit, they sprinkled two-inch roofing tacks in their wake. Later, when they counted the money, they happily split almost

$7000 among them. Karpis later recalled his initiation into bank robbery as a "perfect score."

Freddie and Karpis decided to cool off in St. Paul, Minnesota. While they'd cleaned their tracks in the Mountain View caper, the heat was on Freddie for some killings. He had gunned down West Plains, Missouri, sheriff C.R. Kelly when the lawman tried to question Freddie about a recent store robbery. Later, he drilled five slugs into the back of Chief of Police Manley Jackson during a run-in in Pocaholtas, Arkansas.

Freddie and Karpis took Ma and Arthur Dunlop with them to St. Paul. It didn't take long for Freddie and Karpis to develop a dislike for Dunlop, who was a drunk and a complainer. While the pair kept their fingers nimble with safe-cracking and booze and cigarette hijacking assignments courtesy of St. Paul crime czar Jack Peifer, Dunlop continued to drink bad bootleg booze. Out of boredom, or perhaps resentment, he committed the cardinal sin: he talked too much. One night he ran off his mouth to the wrong people, and soon pictures of Fred Barker and Alvin Karpis, accompanied by details of their activities, appeared in one of the nation's most widely read crime publications, namely, *True Detective Story*.

Fortunately for them, Harry Sawyer, an underworld fixer, heard of an impending police raid and warned the boys. Freddie and Karpis quickly hustled Ma out of the house before the law could move in. But all bets were off with Arthur V. Dunlop.

Freddie later pulled Karpis aside and, with a wild look in his eyes, said, "I'm going to take care of that son of a bitch."

Yet, when Dunlop's corpse turned up floating facedown along the shores of an isolated lake in upstate Wisconsin in 1932, the three bullet holes in his back came neither from Freddie's or Karpis' .45. Dunlop was shot dead by Jack Peifer in appreciation for services rendered.

The boys and Ma went to Kansas City, where on June 17, Freddie, Karpis and five others robbed the Fort Scott Bank. Freddie immediately set the mood for the heist when he started shouting that he was going to kill everyone in the place.

But before they could make their getaway with a take of $47,000, Karpis glanced down the street and saw at least a dozen police officers rushing towards them. Freddie instantly grabbed three girls from the bank and hustled them out the door towards the waiting Hudson. One of the girls passed out before she reached the car, but the bank robbers made the other two stand on the running board as the driver, Tommy Holden, slammed down on the accelerator. A motorcycle cop gave chase, only to narrowly miss being killed when Freddie opened fire with his machine gun.

Following the heist, with the police hot on their trail, Freddie and Karpis once again packed up Ma and headed back to St. Paul. But a lucky break occurred for the gang when three escapees from the Oklahoma State Penitentiary were arrested for carrying a cache of weapons and charged with the Fort Scott Bank raid. Each received prison sentences ranging from 20 to 100 years. Karpis later admitted, without apology, that many innocent men served time for robberies actually committed by the Barker-Karpis Gang.

On September 27, 1932, Doc Barker received a pardon from the Oklahoma State Penitentiary by Governor William H. "Alfalfa Bill" Murray. Ma had again burned the midnight oil petitioning officials to release her son, and she succeeded, but only on condition that Arthur "Doc" Barker leave the state and not return.

That wasn't a concern. Doc wasted no time forging the final link in the Barker-Karpis Gang. On December 16, Doc, Fred, Alvin Karpis and four others, including Lawrence DeVol (an early Karpis mentor and unregenerate killer) and former lawman-turned-outlaw Verne Miller (later a suspected participant

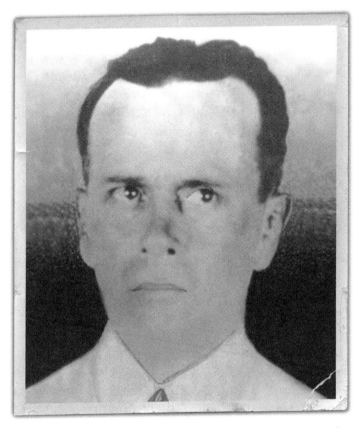

Arthur "Doc" Barker. He survived Ma and two brothers, only to fall victim to his own recklessness when he attempted a break from "The Rock."

in the Kansas City Massacre), robbed the Third Northwestern Bank in Minneapolis. During the raid, the outlaws killed two police officers while making their escape. The gang had begun the process of carrying more firepower than necessary in anticipation of police interference, and in this instance, it was machine-gun fire that ended the lives of the two lawmen.

Despite the killings, the gang was heady with their success. The take from the Third Northwestern Bank job was $20,000. The Barker-Karpis Gang was certainly the most prolific and profitable bank-robbing outfit of the time, successfully hitting 11 banks in 1932. They confined their bank robbing mostly to the Midwest, targeting locations in St. Paul, Chicago, Toledo and Cleveland, and only occasionally extending their operations into Reno, Kansas City and Tulsa.

After enjoying a luxurious winter vacation in Reno, Nevada, the gang went back to work in April 1933. It was a warm, sunny day when Freddie, Doc, Karpis and four experienced gunmen drove into Fairbury, Nebraska. Karpis later recalled that the tight-knit storeowners were a frightened bunch who, anticipating a strike against the town bank, had gathered into vigilante groups.

Before the gang could even make their move, a woman on the street began yelling: "Bank robbers!"

Undaunted, Freddie, Karpis and the others burst into the bank and proceeded to empty out the tills. Aware that the cops and the townspeople were already taking strategic positions along the main street to prevent their escape, the gangsters each selected two hostages to use as shields.

As they burst out the front door, trigger-happy Freddie began firing, taking down a citizen who ran from the courthouse brandishing a Luger. Gang member Earl Christman, who was the first to exit, was wounded by a shot to the collarbone, and in response, turned his machine gun on one of his three hostages, the bank president, firing point-blank into his belly.

"Those sons of bitches!" he screamed out to Karpis. "They pulled apart so that somebody had a clear shot at me!"

As the carnage on the street grew, the gangsters forced their hostages onto the running boards of their car and sped off. Despite the gunplay (in which, miraculously, neither of the wounded citizens died), Fairbury had been a lucrative score. The gang came away with $37,000 in cash and $39,000 in World War I Liberty Bonds.

Earl Christman, however, never did receive his share because he succumbed to his wound at Verne Miller's hideout the following day. He was buried secretly by the gang.

Christman's death was the first fatality suffered by the gang, and it was looked upon as an omen by the others that maybe they were pushing their luck with bank heists. With more and more outlaw gangs springing up across the Midwest, the climate was becoming increasingly dangerous for both professionals and renegades. One story postulates that it was Ma Barker herself who, fearing for her boys' safety, suggested a less risky and potentially more lucrative criminal venture—kidnapping.

Again Alvin Karpis dismissed the claim, insisting that it was St. Paul crime boss Jack Peifer's idea to abduct wealthy brewer William A. Hamm, Jr.

They snatched Hamm on June 15 and immediately dispatched a ransom note demanding $100,000. While the act of kidnapping itself presented little risk, the overall results could have had dire consequences given the country's outrage over the abduction and murder of the Charles Lindbergh baby. Fortunately for the Barker-Karpis Gang, not only was the ransom paid immediately, but the Roger Touhy mob was blamed for the kidnapping. Hamm was released unharmed three days following his abduction 40 miles south of St. Paul.

While enjoying their ill-gotten gains, the gang grew restless for action, and on August 15, robbed the Swift Company payroll of $30,000, and in the process, killed one policeman and wounded another. Seven days later, on August 22, they robbed a Federal Reserve mail truck in Chicago, killing patrolman Miles A. Cunningham and wounding another officer. But the heist was a miserable failure. Their promising take consisted only of sacks containing cancelled checks. To add to their troubles, the next day's headline in the *Chicago Tribune* trumpeted: "Ten Thousand Police Hunt Cop Killers!"

The Barker-Karpis Gang liked to live high, and they each paid big bucks for the privilege. They paid even more for protection. With their last jobs garnering them little more than bad publicity, and with their cash supply rapidly dwindling, Freddie, Doc and Alvin decided to double their score with their next kidnapping.

As with most of the gang's capers, the authorities assumed that Ma had mapped out the myriad details of the plan. But Karpis maintained that nothing could have been further from the truth. The kidnapping of Edward G. Bremer, president of the Commercial State Bank of St. Paul, was the brainchild of their old Syndicate associate, Harry Sawyer.

The grab was set for the morning of January 17, 1934. Other than a brief struggle with Bremer in which Doc was forced to subdue the banker by clubbing him over the head with his pistol, it again appeared that the gang had pulled off a clean kidnapping. The gang promptly received the $200,000 ransom from Bremer's family and released him. But two problems quickly arose. They discovered that the FBI had marked the bills, which were issued in five- and ten-dollar denominations, and their contacts in Reno refused to touch the money. Also, Doc Barker's fingerprint turned up on a carelessly discarded gas can found alongside a Wisconsin road.

Suddenly, the Barker-Karpis Gang was hot news. After years of operating in almost complete anonymity, photos of Freddie and Doc Barker and Alvin Karpis were distributed throughout the country, published not only in such magazines as *Liberty* and *True Detective*, but displayed on thousands of FBI wanted posters.

Freddie and Karpis decided to undergo plastic surgery. While the organized underworld that had previously given protection to the outlaws (for a hefty fee) could no longer provide the same service in view of their now-widespread notoriety, they did recommend a doctor who could perform the surgery.

His name was Joseph P. "Doc" Moran, and he practiced out of a hotel on Irving Park Boulevard in Chicago. As with many underworld physicians, he had a sideline performing abortions for gangsters' lady friends, and one such operation had landed him a term at Joliet.

Freddie and Karpis were dubious about subjecting themselves to a procedure that promised a long and painful recovery (not to mention uncertain results), but practicality outweighed their doubts. Crimes previously attributed to other lesser gangs were now being credited to the Barker-Karpis outfit. So Freddie paid Moran $500 and Karpis paid $750 for the operation, which Karpis later likened to a form of medieval torture.

The fingerprint removal was particularly painful as Moran scraped the end of each finger with a scalpel "like he was sharpening a pencil." For all that they endured, Freddie and Alvin were bitterly disappointed to discover that their appearances hadn't changed much.

One night while twitching in excruciating pain from an infected thumb, Freddie shouted, "I'm going to kill that guy as soon as I can hold a gun!"

Freddie and Alvin had hoped to be rid of Doc Moran following their ordeal, but such was not the case. While recovering from their surgery in an apartment house in Toledo, the boys were forced to call upon Moran when an associate named Fred Campbell demanded medical attention after being bitten by a dog that he feared had rabies.

Moran decided to hang around Toledo for a while. He fancied himself a ladies' man, but he was also a drunk, and the combination proved lethal. He was a regular at a local whorehouse where, fueled with potent spirits, he would brag about his surgical ability and how invaluable his skills were to criminals on the run from the law.

"I have this gang right here in the palm of my hand," he slurred one night to the bordello madam.

He was, of course, referring to Freddie Barker and Alvin Karpis. When Freddie heard directly from the madam about Moran's big talk, he was uncharacteristically contained.

But after Moran had not been seen for a lengthy period, Freddie confided to Karpis: "Doc and I shot the son of a bitch. Anybody who talks to whores is much too dangerous to live. We dug a hole in Michigan and dropped him in and covered the hole with lime. I don't think anyone's gonna come across Doc Moran again."

Doc Moran wasn't the only underworld associate who posed a threat to the gang once their criminal past became public. Barker-Karpis fringe members Fred Goetz, Jess Doyle and underworld contact William Harrison had each broken the gang's trust and were likewise eliminated in particularly grisly fashion. Goetz's face was obliterated by several close-range shotgun blasts, and Harrison, after being lured to a barn in Illinois, was shot and doused with gasoline before both he and the barn were set ablaze.

As Karpis later stated: "That was my friend Freddie Barker. All business."

Trying desperately to stay ahead of the law, the boys, with Ma in tow, moved south and spent time both in Miami and Cuba. The FBI was coming down hard on the nation's criminals, and it seemed that each day newscaster Lowell Thomas announced the death or capture of another outlaw contemporary.

Doc Barker stayed in Chicago. On the night of January 8, 1935, as he and his girlfriend were leaving their apartment near Lake Michigan, ace G-man Melvin Purvis and a team of federal agents intercepted him. Unbeknownst to Doc, gang member "Slim Gray" Gibson had informed on him.

As he was frisked by agents, Purvis asked him, "Where's your gun?"

Doc merely smirked. "Home," he replied. "And ain't that a hell of a place for it?"

Purvis took Doc to FBI headquarters at the Bankers' Building in downtown Chicago, where he was handcuffed to a chair and grilled relentlessly for eight days and nights. But Doc Barker adhered to the code of the underworld and refused to divulge the whereabouts of any of his fellow gang members.

Purvis later wrote: "He sat in a chair, his jaw clenched, and looked straight ahead. He was not impressive-looking; only his eyes told the story of an innate savagery."

Unaware of Doc's apprehension, Freddie and Ma were enjoying themselves in secluded surroundings at their rented lakeside cottage at Lake Weir, Florida, where reportedly, Freddie's favorite pastime was machine-gunning alligators. Alvin Karpis spent a few days at their "small paradise" before leaving to be with his common-law wife Dolores Delaney, who was expecting their first child.

Alvin recalled seeing a definite change in Ma before his departure. Where previously she'd never had any use for any of her boys' female companions, she was now excited about the upcoming birth and even offered to help out with household chores while Dolores was tending to the baby.

Karpis' decision to leave proved a lucky move for the outlaw because Melvin Purvis and his squad were closing in on Ma and Freddie. The G-men had come upon a map of Florida highlighting the Ocala region while searching Doc's Chicago apartment.

On January 16, federal and local authorities surrounded the Lake Weir resort. According to the official report, an agent named Connelly knocked on the door of the house and informed Kate Barker that they were there to arrest her son. Ma played along and went to fetch Freddie, who had already taken up position next to an upstairs window. He responded with a burst from his machine gun. Connelly dove for cover while fellow agents opened fire.

Later witnesses claimed that it was Ma herself who was heard giving her son the command: "All right. Go ahead!"

A six-hour machine-gun battle ensued, ending only when the agents had exhausted their supply of ammunition. As the minutes ticked by, an eerie silence descended over the grounds. No further gunfire erupted from inside the bullet-torn, wood-frame house.

Agents sent an elderly Negro handyman named Willie Woodbury who worked for the Barkers inside to check out the situation. Moments later he called out from an upstairs window, "Dey's dead, boss! Dey's dead!"

Exactly how and when Ma and Freddie died has never been determined. The FBI agents pumped so much lead into the house for such a prolonged period of time that it is likely that the Barkers were dead long before the shooting finally ceased.

Their bodies were found in an upstairs bedroom. Freddie, with 11 bullet wounds piercing his body, had obviously gone down fighting. He was still holding his Thompson submachine gun. Ma had taken three gunshot wounds, including one directly to the heart. A .300 gas-operated rifle with 40 of its 94 rounds spent lay next to her corpse.

Ma's fatal bullet wound led to speculation that perhaps she had taken her own life. Despite her earlier pronouncement following son Herman's suicide: "A Barker don't do things like that," it is possible that Ma witnessed Freddie's death, and being devastated and realizing the futility of her situation, just chose to end it all.

However she died, Kate Barker did not leave the world in the state of poverty in which she'd entered it—$10,200 was found in her handbag. The saga of the Bloody Barkers was at its climax.

Thirty-six-year-old Doc Barker was sentenced to life imprisonment at Alcatraz (where he was assigned #268) for the Bremer kidnapping. Although he was soon reunited with Alvin Karpis on The Rock, Doc resumed his restless pattern of planning and executing prison breaks, even from the seemingly escape-proof fortress. At night on June 13, 1939, Doc and five other convicts made it over the prison walls and rushed towards the rocky shoreline of San Francisco Bay, where they hastily began constructing a makeshift raft. A dense fog enveloped them, and the steady roar of the surf drowned out the sound of their rushed efforts. As searchlights speared about them, Doc remained steadfast in his purpose.

Finally, he was pinpointed in the whitish light. Then came the command: "Barker! Throw your hands in the air!"

Doc sneered and continued with what he was doing. Seconds later, as he waded out into the raging tide, he was felled by a volley of gunfire from the guard tower. He was still alive as he was pulled from the frigid waters but refused medical aid.

His dying words were: "I'm all shot to hell."

Lloyd Barker, whose lengthy imprisonment for his aborted postal robbery attempt precluded his involvement with the Barker-Karpis Gang, was paroled from Leavenworth in 1947 and went to work as the assistant manager of a snack shop in Colorado. While he was apparently content leading a law-abiding life, he completed the Barker circle of violence when his wife shot him to death in 1949.

George Barker outlived his wife and all four of his sons. The old man dutifully claimed their bodies and buried them side by side in an open field near the filling station that he operated in Welch, Ohio.

So who was Ma Barker? If Alvin Karpis and others are to be believed, her notorious reputation grew only after her death and was the result of media manipulation forged and perpetuated by the FBI in an attempt to justify an unjust killing.

As the last survivor of the Barker-Karpis Gang, Alvin Karpis summed up Kate "Ma" Barker in his own words: "Ma was superstitious, gullible, simple, cantankerous and generally law-abiding."

Has history wrongly judged Ma Barker? If she truly was neither the leader of a pack of criminal mad dogs nor a criminal herself, then she just had the misfortune to nurture sons born with the killer instinct. And if such is the case, then the only real crime of which Kate Barker is guilty is having an excess of motherly love.

CHAPTER SIX

Alvin "Old Creepy" Karpis

(1908–1979)

"My profession was robbing banks, knocking off payrolls and kidnapping rich men. I was good at it. Maybe the best in North America."

–Alvin Karpis

ALVIN "OLD CREEPY" KARPIS not only enjoyed the longest professional run of the Depression Day Desperadoes (1931–36), he also holds the distinction of surviving the era, outliving his contemporaries and having the opportunity to tell his side of the story. And if his accounts are to be believed, they blast .45-caliber holes into the fabric of criminal history.

Karpis was the last of big-name Public Enemies. He committed every crime in the book (with the possible exception of murder), and even as he mellowed in his later years, he never apologized for his past. His attitude was always: "What happened, happened."

He was a controversial figure during his career, and he became outspoken when, after serving 33 years in prison (25 of which were spent at Alcatraz, longer than any other inmate in the penitentiary's history), he was finally granted parole and returned to his native Canada. Karpis published his autobiography in 1971 and became a popular radio and television talk show guest. He spoke freely about his criminal exploits

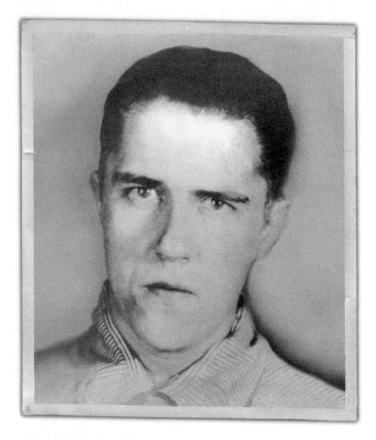

Alvin "Old Creepy" Karpis survived both the era and the longest stretch ever served by an inmate at Alcatraz.

and of his recollections of the other top gangsters of the time—those he liked and respected (John Dillinger, Baby Face Nelson, Pretty Boy Floyd and, of course, Ma Barker and her boys) and those he had little or no use for (Bonnie and Clyde and Machine Gun Kelly).

Alvin Karpis was a veritable encyclopedia of crime. He crossed paths with everyone from Al Capone to Charles Manson, who had aspirations as a musician and wanted Karpis to teach him to play the guitar.

Karpis' most famous association, however, was with the Barker Gang, and he vehemently denied that Ma Barker ever played a significant role in their criminal careers. Karpis had no reason to lie, not when he always spoke with such brutal honesty about the wild ways of Doc and Freddie Barker and himself.

Was it with brutal honesty that Karpis made his most controversial claim concerning FBI chief J. Edgar Hoover and his supposed personal capture of Alvin Karpis? The official FBI version and Karpis' account differ dramatically. Karpis remained virtually mute on the subject throughout all his years in prison. But following his release and deportation, he finally broke his silence, publicly challenging the validity of FBI records, stating that Hoover's version of his arrest was totally false. A convicted Public Enemy attacking the integrity of the Federal Bureau of Investigation would appear to be a fool's move, unless he was firm in his conviction. And Karpis really had nothing to gain by opening himself to controversy at that stage of his life.

Certainly Karpis harbored animosity towards Hoover. He believed that it was because of the Bureau chief's influence that he spent 33 years behind bars even though he was eligible for parole after serving 15. (Hoover had supposedly told Karpis that he would "rot to death in Alcatraz.") And Karpis was just as resentful that Hoover's restored and glorified reputation during a tenuous period in the 1930s was achieved through a bogus act of heroism at Karpis' expense. Perhaps Karpis himself provided the answer when he merely said that it was time to set the record straight.

"I made that son of a bitch," he remarked.

Hoover was equally blunt when expressing his contempt for Karpis, referring to him as a "dirty yellow rat."

Hoover had reason to despise Alvin Karpis, who had a longer and generally more profitable career than any other outlaw of the time, including John Dillinger. Karpis' success shed a negative light on the performance of the FBI, which hitherto had enjoyed a prestigious resurgence of public confidence because of its resourceful work in eliminating the nation's gangster element.

There is no doubt that luck played a role in Karpis' criminal longevity (given that lesser maverick gangs were often "pinched" for crimes committed by the Barker-Karpis outfit). But Alvin Karpis was also a careful and meticulous criminal who knew how to use his brain. The story goes that even during his final years in Spain, just for his own amusement, he would often figure out ways to break into a particularly attractive bank.

A former partner-in-crime named Fred Hunter described Karpis as "super-smart." Nor was Karpis himself modest when discussing his abilities, admitting that, under different circumstances, he might have had a successful career in law or any other profession that demanded "style and brains and a cool, hard way of handling yourself." He certainly had little doubt that he could have held the highest job in any line of police detection work.

"I outthought, outwitted and just plain defeated enough cops and G-men in my time to recognize that I was more knowledgeable about crime than any of them, including J. Edgar Hoover."

Sometimes the mere flip of a coin determines a person's destiny, and for young Albin Karpowicz of Montreal, Canada, the coin landed "tails."

"I was 10 years old and already on my way to being Public Enemy Number One," he later wrote

Albin Karpowicz was born in 1908, the second of four children and the only son of John and Anna Karpowicz, Lithuanian immigrants who moved to Topeka, Kansas, when Albin was still young.

John Karpowicz worked hard to provide for his family, both running their farm and working full time for the Santa Fe Railroad. He tried to instill the same work ethic in his children, but Albin had little interest in backbreaking manual labor. He preferred picking up the occasional dollar running errands for the whores, pimps, bootleggers and petty gamblers who operated in Topeka.

"I just liked the action," he explained.

Two of the lasting influences in his life were the shortening and simplifying of his name to Alvin Karpis by a grade school teacher and his association with 18-year-old Arthur Witchey, who arrived in Topeka straight out of reformatory school. The impressionable Alvin idolized Witchey, and when the older boy asked Alvin to help him break into a grocery store, the 10-year-old eagerly agreed.

Impressed by how easy it was to make a dishonest dollar, Alvin spent the next five years honing his skills with break and entries and other petty theft. While the take was usually small, Alvin prided himself on never once getting caught.

His crime career was briefly interrupted when his father moved the family to Chicago. At age 15, Karpis made an effort at honest work, taking jobs as an errand boy and later as a shipping clerk for a drug company. Alvin quit the latter job when he developed a mild heart problem and was advised by his physician to find a less strenuous line of work. Alvin, although amused at the irony, followed his doctor's advice and returned to Topeka and his criminal pursuits. He and a friend operated a hamburger stand that served as a front for fencing stolen goods and supplying bootleg booze to thirsty patrons. Karpis also sidelined with warehouse break-ins.

He'd always had a fascination with trains and began riding the rails, traveling throughout the South and Midwest. Ironically, it was because of this diversion and not one of his more overt criminal pursuits that Karpis was arrested for the first time. He was picked up by a railroad bull in Florida, charged as a vagrant and slapped with a 30-day sentence on a chain gang.

Upon his release, Karpis traveled to Kansas, where he was nabbed by the cops while breaking into a warehouse. Because he'd already done time, he got the unusually stiff sentence of 5 to 10 years at the Hutchinson Kansas State Reformatory.

Hutchinson was rough, but the 5'6", 120-pound Karpis had already developed a tough exterior. He also benefited from his prison experience because it brought him into contact with fellow inmate Lawrence DeVol. DeVol was a hardcore case, but he took a liking to the teenage Karpis and became his mentor in burglary procedure. Then, in 1929, three years into his sentence, Karpis joined DeVol and two other cons in breaking out of Hutchinson, using tools obtained from the prison workshop to saw their way through a barred door to freedom.

Karpis stuck with DeVol, and the two embarked on a burglary spree throughout Kansas, Oklahoma and Missouri. They managed to elude the law for almost a year, until DeVol was nabbed in Chicago and sent back to Hutchinson.

DeVol was wise to the system and asked for a transfer to the Kansas State Penitentiary in Lansing, where time was deducted for inmates who volunteered to work in the coal mine. When he was released after only months, DeVol again hooked up with Karpis, who in the interim had tried to appease his parents by once more attempting honest work as a baker's helper. The pair picked up where they'd left off.

While the two worked mainly as a team, occasionally DeVol chose to go off on a job alone or with another partner.

Whether by choice or by accident, on two of these forays men were killed. One night while robbing a store in Perry, Oklahoma, DeVol chose to confront a night watchman head-on, taking him down with a .45 bullet to the jugular. In Lexington, Michigan, DeVol and another burglar had just robbed a combination pool hall and restaurant when a policeman jumped them in the alley. They exchanged gunfire, and the cop died. A gleam of madness shone in DeVol's eyes when he recounted these stories to Karpis. Karpis realized that his pal Larry DeVol possessed a frightening bloodlust. While Karpis did not approve of his partner's methods, he continued to look upon DeVol as a mentor and would never question his technique.

Times were hard for everyone in 1930, even professional thieves. DeVol often bemoaned the fact that their scores netted them little cash. On their way to rob a downtown pool hall in Kansas City, suspicious police stopped them, discovered their burglary tools and hauled them in for questioning. As Karpis remembered, their third-degree methods included round-the-clock beatings and other "unique" forms of persuasion.

"This one hefty cop had a trick of putting four pencils between all the fingers and thumb of one of my hands and then squeezing as hard as he could. Then he'd stand behind me and press his thumbs with all his might behind my ears."

When the police finally discovered their identities, and Karpis was returned to Hutchinson to finish out his sentence, a guard remarked, "Karpis and DeVol took the worst beatings the cops ever gave anyone in Kansas City."

Karpis followed DeVol's example and requested a transfer to Lansing, where he immediately volunteered for work in the coal mine to have his sentence reduced. He also "bought" time from some of the old-timers who were more interested in money than freedom.

Lansing would be the most significant prison stay of Karpis' career because it was there that he met Freddie Barker. Freddie had a tougher rep than Karpis, but he felt that Alvin had the makings of a potential partner, and when they got together in Joplin, Missouri, following their respective releases, they tested the waters with penny-ante burglaries, including pawnshops and clothing stores.

Karpis and Freddie bonded like brothers. It was actually Freddie who coined Karpis' famous nickname "Old Creepy" because of his friend's sinister smile and oddly penetrating stare. Karpis and Ma were also close, and the Barkers soon regarded Alvin as part of the family. Karpis recalled that in some ways he was more like a son to Ma than her own boys, often taking her to movies (which she loved) and even accompanying her to the 1933 Chicago World's Fair.

When Doc Barker was paroled from prison, Freddie, Doc and Alvin formed the nucleus of the Barker-Karpis Gang. Fringe members included: Karpis' old mentor Lawrence DeVol (shot and killed in 1936 in Enid, Oklahoma, by the chief of police following a gun battle in which he'd killed two police officers), Jess Doyle (later murdered by Freddie), Earl Christman (killed in the Fairbury bank hold-up), Fred Goetz (aka "Shotgun Ziegler," a reputed participant in the St. Valentine's Day Massacre and later executed by Freddie for suspected duplicity) and Frank "Jelly" Nash (whose planned escape from federal officers precipitated the Kansas City Massacre).

The gang specialized in rural bank holdups, which were always planned around wheat harvest time when the farmers deposited large sums into their accounts. Karpis remembered some "withdrawals" bringing them upwards of $100,000.

Because the gang accumulated so much money and mostly managed to stay out of the spotlight, they could afford to be well protected by the national crime cartel, the Syndicate, through its major branches in St. Louis, Kansas City and Chicago. In each city they could fence ransom money through crooked political contacts (who naturally retained a large percentage for their efforts), even handing cash over to various trusted officials from whom they would then draw sums as needed, much like a bank.

Karpis couldn't help but become jaded by such corruption and later remarked: "Everybody had a price."

Still, as long as the gang didn't become reckless, they were looked after. Nor did Karpis' reputation go unnoticed by the organized underworld. At a time when Karpis was particularly "hot," the Syndicate approached him and offered him protection and $250 a week to work as an enforcer. Karpis, who considered himself a thief, not a hood, politely refused the offer.

But Karpis' choice to remain independent was becoming risky, especially with Freddie's growing dependence on alcohol and narcotics. Freddie was getting reckless and paranoid, his unpredictable behavior reaching a violent climax in the fall of 1933 when the gang decided to stick up the South St. Paul Post Office.

The simple plan involved robbing three employees as they carried money from the post office to the bank. The procedure seemed easy enough, except that two cars with policemen would follow closely.

Whereas Freddie had always been impulsive but not careless, on the morning of the heist he suddenly appeared on the street with his machine gun blazing. Like a scene out of a gangster movie, one of the police cars was hit and careened out of control, jumping the curb, then ricocheting off a building and back onto the road. Freddie kept firing, his shots wild, blasting chunks out of buildings and even hitting a streetcar that came upon the scene.

By now the police and bank guards joined in the exchange of gunfire. Freddie's relentless shooting brought down two police officers. One of the gang, Chuck Fitzgerald, caught a bullet in the hip and had to drag himself to the getaway car. The gangsters squealed away under a barrage of gunfire with $3000 in coins and $30,000 in paper money. In their wake, they left one dead police officer and another wounded lawman.

Following the incident and the Federal Reserve fiasco, the gang ventured into kidnapping, pulling off the successful grabs of William Hamm and Edward Bremer, although marked bills and carelessness on the part of Doc Barker soon brought the Barker-Karpis Gang to public attention and, more seriously, made them FBI targets.

Following Doc Barker's capture and the deaths of Freddie and Ma in Florida, Alvin Karpis found himself the subject of the greatest manhunt in history. He had inherited the mantle of Public Enemy Number One, and J. Edgar Hoover intensified the Bureau's efforts to apprehend him. According to legend, Karpis responded by writing notes to Hoover threatening to kill him. Karpis denied ever sending such messages; he believed the messages were all part of an elaborate publicity ploy designed to further boost Hoover's image when the director publicly declared that he would personally bring Alvin Karpis to justice.

Hoover was under extreme criticism at this time. Senator Kenneth McKellar of Tennessee in particular had taken him to task. While his agents (particularly the fastidious Melvin Purvis) were being touted as heroes for their role in bringing down the gangster menace, Hoover, the country's top G-man, had yet to make an arrest himself. Hoover understood that by personally putting the cuffs on the nation's last named Public Enemy, he would restore his reputation both to his critics and the public in general.

Karpis had undergone painful plastic surgery, but the results were not satisfactory. He tried to add to his disguise

Melvin Purvis and J. Edgar Hoover. The gang-busting achievements of ace G-man Melvin Purvis prompted FBI director J. Edgar Hoover's vow that he would personally capture Alvin Karpis. Hoover resented Purvis and even issued the following statement: "No one employee of this division can be responsible for the successful termination of any one case. Through cooperative efforts a case is broken." Hoover conspired to have Purvis resign from the FBI and also prevented Purvis from obtaining employment in any other field of law enforcement. Purvis never quite recovered from Hoover's "betrayal." Although he enjoyed moderate success as narrator of Post Toasties' *Melvin Purvis' Law and Order Patrol*, Purvis died of a self-inflicted bullet wound to the head on February 29, 1960, at age 56. Ironically, the gun was the same automatic pistol Purvis used to hunt Dillinger and Floyd.

by cropping his hair short and wearing owl-lensed eyeglasses, which gave the gangster an oddly sinister academic look. Unfortunately, no amount of masquerade could effectively alter his basic appearance.

After a brief stay in Miami, Karpis and Harry Campbell headed to Atlantic City, where they had earlier sent their girls to arrange lodgings for them. But Karpis was uneasy in Atlantic City. Both he and Campbell felt that they were constantly being tailed. To add to Karpis' stress, Dolores was eight months pregnant with their child.

They had taken a room at the Danmore Hotel, where early one morning they were awakened by frantic knocking at their door. A woman named Mrs. Morley, who with her husband ran the hotel, had come to warn Karpis that five detectives were waiting downstairs.

When Karpis peered into the lobby to see for himself, Mrs. Morley began screaming, "Here's one of 'em! Here he is!"

Karpis stayed cool as the armed cops rushed up the stairs towards him.

Feigning ignorance, he said, "What is all this?" He spoke in a voice loud enough to alert Harry Campbell who was in an adjoining room.

"Don't point those guns at me," Karpis protested vehemently. "I haven't done anything."

The cops knew Campbell was in the next room and ordered him to come out.

"He's probably hung over; we got a little drunk last night," Karpis explained. He then offered to go inside and bring him out. The cops agreed.

Karpis' ruse worked. As soon as he opened the door, he threw himself aside as Campbell let loose with his machine gun. One cop was wounded by flying plaster and was rushed down the stairs by the others. Karpis ran back to his own room, threw on trousers and an overcoat and grabbed his automatic. Dolores had been hit in the leg by Campbell's wild shooting, and Karpis hurriedly fashioned a bandage for her out of a strip of bedding before herding both women down to the back exit. He told them to wait beneath the stairwell while he and Campbell went for the car.

The cops spotted them instantly and fired on them as they raced towards the garage where their Buick was parked. They were unable to locate their car, but Karpis came upon a new Pontiac with a full tank of gas and keys in the ignition.

Leaping inside, Karpis threw the car into gear and floored it, roaring out onto the street. But he missed the turn to the alley where Dolores and Wynona were waiting, and he had to swing back and forth down streets and alleys trying to locate them. Finally, Karpis had no choice but to leave them behind. He careened down alleys until he ran into a dead end. He glanced behind him only to realize that police officers had rushed in to block their exit onto the street.

"To hell with it, we'll run right through," Karpis said to Campbell. "Get the gun ready."

Campbell leaned out the car window and aimed his machine gun at the cops as Karpis swung the car into a 180° turn, floored the pedal and barreled straight towards them. At almost the last minute, Karpis spotted an intersecting alley and quickly swerved into it. He and Campbell finally got away when they spun out onto a highway leading away from town.

Their narrow escape wasn't the end of their problems. They now had to switch vehicles. A description of the '34 Pontiac they were driving was probably already being dispatched to police units throughout the state. Near Allentown, Pennsylvania, they noticed a 1934 Plymouth emblazoned with medical emblems on the rear bumper. A doctor's car would provide them with the perfect cover, and Karpis immediately pulled alongside the Plymouth.

Harry Campbell shouted out the passenger window, "State police. Pull over. We want to talk to you."

The driver, Dr. Horace Hunsicker, complied and was then kidnapped while the gangsters commandeered his car to leave the state. Hunsicker was released unharmed in Wadsworth, Ohio, and Karpis slipped him 50 bucks for his cooperation.

The criminals then headed into Toledo, one of the mob-run cities that provided a safe haven for Karpis when things got too hot. There, both he and Campbell laid low at a bordello run by a madam named Edith Barry. Karpis spent his time reading newspapers to keep abreast of developments. He discovered that Dolores had been taken into custody by the FBI and had given birth to their son while in hospital detention quarters in Philadelphia. The baby was given over to the care of Karpis' parents, and both Dolores and Wynona Burdette were then sent back to Florida to face charges of harboring criminals. Eventually, Dolores was sentenced to a lengthy prison term at a Michigan woman's facility.

Karpis later wrote about the trials that the women in his life endured: "They all found out at one time or another that I was a crook and chose to stick by me. I loved each one of them."

Karpis needed to stay busy if for no other reason than to keep his mind occupied. Through an associate, Fred Hunter, Karpis and Campbell planned a payroll robbery at the Youngstown Sheet and Tube Plant in Warren, Ohio. Hunter estimated that their take would be close to $100,000.

It would be a simple job, but with so many of the top heist men either dead or in prison, Karpis was forced to seek out second-rate talent. Finally, they teamed with a small-time burglar named Joe Rich, who was a hophead,* but who

---

*Hophead was a slang term at the time used to describe a drug addict.

promised to keep his habit under control during the planning and execution of the heist. On April 25, 1935, they intercepted the mail truck containing the payroll shipment and carted away $72,000 in cash.

Then, like a welcome echo from the past, two other criminals were identified as the robbers by the mail truck driver and arrested for the crime. Hoover, however, knew who the real culprits were and was incensed at Karpis' audacity. He took the robbery as a personal affront, given the Bureau's well-publicized manhunt for the gangster.

Karpis realized that his glory days were fading and decided to make what might be his last heist the most imaginative and spectacular yet. Like many other outlaws of the time, Karpis patterned his exploits after the desperadoes of the Old West. He decided to pull off a train robbery, specifically the mail train that carried payrolls from the Federal Reserve in Cleveland to small Ohio towns.

"I thought of all the great bandits of the Old West," he later said, "the James brothers, the Dalton boys and all the rest of them. They all knocked over trains at some point in their careers, and I was going to pull the same stunt."

On payroll day, the train carried enough cash to pay the weekly salaries of all the hard-working mill workers throughout Ohio's industrial centers.

Karpis still had only slim pickings for recruits, but he traveled between Cleveland and Toledo, selecting a man named Brock; Ben Grayson, an older and experienced robber recently released from prison; and an old Barker-Karpis stalwart, Sam Coker.

Grayson was dubious. "Just one thing," he said. "Who the hell robs a train in this day and age?"

Karpis calmly laid out the plan, conceived with brilliant criminal strategy, each detail mapped out. His men were convinced. He had even arranged for a pilot to fly them to Hot Springs, Arkansas, immediately after the heist.

Karpis thought he had all his bases covered, but he hadn't counted on the questionable habits of some of his gang. When Sam Coker collapsed one day, they discovered that he was suffering from gonorrhea. Karpis had lost his lookout at the train depot. Karpis then learned that the FBI, anticipating a daring move by the outlaw, had peppered the Cleveland area with agents.

Karpis wasn't deterred. But when veteran Ben Grayson appeared ready for work looking like a villain out of a silent movie, replete with a long drooping mustache, Karpis remarked, "For Chissake, Ben, don't move too close to the people on the platform. You'll scare the hell out of them."

Grayson refused to remove his disguise.

The robbery was set for 2:45 PM. When Erie Train No. 622 hissed into the small station at Garrettsville, Ohio, the men went into action. Fred Hunter stayed in the parking lot to guard their escape route. Grayson climbed into the engineer's cab and held the two trainmen at gunpoint. Brandishing a shotgun, Brock watched the station's platform. Karpis and Campbell approached the mail car. Its heavy door slid open, and the machine-gun-wielding outlaws greeted the two clerks.

Campbell grinned, "Howdy, boys. Fine day for a robbery."

The clerks immediately dashed for cover among the mail sacks at the back of the car. Karpis ordered them to come out, and when they refused, threw an unlit stick of dynamite inside.

He promised, "I'm going to heave another stick in there, and this one'll be burning. You've got five seconds to come out."

He began counting. The quavering clerks reappeared, and in their company was a third fellow—a big, heavyset black man who did not seem to be afraid.

"You can't do this, man," he said to Karpis. "Get off with that gun."

Karpis raised the barrel of the machine gun up over their heads and pulled the trigger. The shot didn't go off, but the men were convinced of the gangster's sincerity and threw their hands in the air. Still, the senior clerk wouldn't identify for Karpis which of the many mail sacks held the payroll.

Karpis knew that each second counted, so he leveled his machine gun at the clerk. He reminded him that there would be another train coming down the line in just a few minutes, and unless the guy cooperated, he'd just keep everyone in place and stand by to watch the resulting collision.

Karpis wasn't a murderer; he just knew how to be persuasive when he needed to be.

The clerk recanted, but unfortunately for the robbers, the mail sack containing the payroll for Youngstown was not in the mail car. At that point, Karpis was ready to pull the trigger on the old man. But the clerk quickly showed him the ledger proving that the Youngstown payroll had been delivered the day before.

Karpis was livid, but there wasn't much he could do about it. He and Campbell grabbed the Warren payroll along with five other mail sacks that they hoped were filled with something more substantial than letters and demanded that the clerks load them into the back of their Plymouth.

"Hey, I ain't gonna help you rob the train," the black man protested.

"The hell you ain't," retorted Harry Campbell, as he kicked him in the backside.

When the gang checked out their loot later at a cottage in Port Clinton, they were disappointed to find that their anticipated $200,000 payday amounted to just $34,000. Karpis tried to remain philosophical. At least he'd accomplished what he had set out to do.

The Stinson flight that Karpis had arranged transported him and Campbell south to Hot Springs, Arkansas, where he made a present of the airplane to pilot Al Zetzer along with an extra $500 to get rid of their car back in Port Clinton. Karpis spent the next few days cooling off at the whorehouse run by his new girlfriend, Grace Goldstein.

With the FBI trailing him throughout Ohio, Karpis decided to take Grace on a vacation to Paris, Texas, to visit her brother, Leonard. Paris was one town that didn't have a local FBI office. The town was one of the most poverty-stricken Karpis had seen in his travels. He would later describe it as "a share-cropper's nightmare." Their stay in Paris was brief, and Karpis was glad to move on.

Karpis was never in one place for long. During the months from autumn 1935 to early winter 1936, Alvin and Fred Hunter kept moving through Arkansas, Florida, Mississippi and Tennessee. It was not only the FBI who doggedly pursued the gangster, but also the postal authorities, who had set their sights on Karpis ever since the Garrettsville payroll robbery.

And it seemed that the postal people were having more luck than the G-men in tracing the stolen money. Their efforts led them to Ohio where they hauled in Brock, who spilled everything he knew, including all the details of the train heist and Karpis' getaway by plane. Additional pressure mounted when Hoover guaranteed a $5000 reward to anyone who had information concerning Karpis' whereabouts.

Karpis learned firsthand how serious the situation had become when Grace briefly visited a house they had rented on Malvern Road, between Hot Springs and Malvern, Arkansas. Believing Karpis was inside, the FBI waited until Grace had exited the premises before launching a barrage of gunfire that destroyed the house.

But the assault on the house on Malvern Road spelled more trouble for J. Edgar Hoover. The wealthy owner of the property, a man named Woodcock, happened to be a close friend of U.S. Senator Joe Robinson. Hoover was called upon to explain the actions of his men on the floor of the Senate, and the humiliating experience no doubt compounded his already festering hatred for Alvin Karpis. Meanwhile, Karpis enjoyed one of his few moments of levity while reading of Hoover's predicament.

Because their last heist had been so disappointing, Karpis was already planning new scores, including a possible payroll robbery at a construction project called Pickwick Dam in Mississippi and even another train robbery in Iuka in the same state.

Karpis was living in New Orleans, holed up in an apartment on St. Charles Boulevard. He couldn't seem to relax and neither could Freddie Hunter. Both felt that they were under constant surveillance whenever they went out. Karpis attributed their anxiety to nerves, but he couldn't afford to be careless, so he watched for any suspicious-looking people.

On May 1, Karpis was still edgy and had left the apartment a few times to run mindless errands. Towards evening he asked Hunter to drive him to the garage where he had taken his car to be serviced. It was hot, and Karpis conceded to the temperature by leaving his jacket behind, along with his automatic.

Karpis slid behind the wheel of the '36 Plymouth Coupe, while Freddie sat on the passenger side. Just as Karpis pushed the key into the ignition, a car screeched to a halt directly in front of them.

According to the official FBI version, Karpis, realizing that the jig was up, made a desperate move towards a rifle lying on the backseat. It was then that J. Edgar Hoover himself threw open the car door and clamped a beefy hand down on the outlaw's outstretched arm. At the same time, an agent named Connelly dove into the car from the passenger side and likewise restrained Karpis.

For years this version of Karpis' capture (which was also detailed in Don Whitehead's "official" documentation of the Bureau's early history, *The FBI Story*) was accepted as fact.

Hoover was regarded as a hero, and never again would his bravery be questioned. Hoover received an immediate pay raise to $10,000 annually and remained in office until his death in 1972.

During Karpis' long incarceration he was frequently asked about his arrest. His reply to questioning officials was always: "Why don't you ask Mr. Hoover?"

But with the release of his 1971 autobiography, *The Alvin Karpis Story*, he finally decided to divulge his version of events. He wrote that he barely had time to recover from the suddenness of the car cutting in front of them before five men burst out from all four doors, and he felt the barrel of a rifle hit against his head.

"All right, Karpis, just keep your hands on the steering wheel," he was ordered.

Karpis saw that he was completely surrounded, guns aimed at him from every direction. The scene quickly lost all sense of order, with crowds of curious bystanders gathering around and agents barking contradictory orders at Karpis. With all the attention focused on Karpis, Freddie Hunter managed to ease himself from the Plymouth and walk casually down the street before a vigilant citizen yelled out a window to the agents, one of whom quickly collared Hunter.

Karpis later learned that he'd narrowly escaped a federal ambush. Twenty lethally armed agents were preparing to burst into the apartment with guns blazing, when Karpis surprised them by walking out onto the street.

Once Karpis was safely in custody (his hands bound with his own necktie because, incredibly, none of the agents had remembered to bring handcuffs) and a semblance of order restored, an agent called out: "We've got him. It's all clear, Chief."

Karpis remembered two men, one instantly recognizable as J. Edgar Hoover, walking around the side of the apartment building, waiting to take the credit for the arrest.

"We called them the 'Gold Dust' twins," Karpis later laughed, referring to Hoover and his right-hand man Clyde Tolson.

Hoover flew with Karpis to St. Paul, Minnesota, where the gangster was to stand trial for the kidnapping of William Hamm. The director continually baited Karpis, at one point referring to him by the hated term "hoodlum." Hoover demanded immediate cooperation from Karpis and promised that unless he complied completely, Hoover would see Karpis electrocuted.

Karpis was denied a lawyer (a lawyer had been promised to him by Hoover on condition that he sign a waiver allowing agents to transport him directly to St. Paul to stand trial on kidnapping charges) and spent days undergoing intense interrogation. He was cuffed to a radiator, threatened, denied basic requests and was punched awake each time he dared to doze off. His only satisfaction came from the occasional dig directed at the ineptitude of various FBI operations of which he had inside knowledge.

Then one morning, a half-delirious Karpis was cleaned up, fed and allowed some rest prior to his appearance before the county commissioner. On the afternoon of May 6, 1936, the deputy court clerk asked Karpis if he was prepared to make bond, set at $500,000, the highest bail ever charged against a criminal in United States history.

Karpis' response was quoted in papers throughout the country: "Well, hardly."

Alvin Karpis pleaded guilty to four counts of kidnapping, two each for William Hamm and Edward Bremer. The U.S. District Attorney promised him that by uttering a guilty plea, he would not only be spared the death penalty, but that his sentence would allow him to apply for parole after serving a term of years. On the day of sentencing, Karpis' optimism was crushed when the judge handed him life.

Karpis entered The Rock on August 7, 1936 (Prisoner #325). Twenty-five years later on April 7, 1962, he was transferred to

McNeil Island Penitentiary at Puget Sound, Washington, to serve out the last stretch of his sentence. Karpis finally saw freedom in 1969.

He enjoyed a brief, if controversial, celebrity in his native Canada due to the publication of his memoirs and many subsequent interviews. Besides freely discussing Hoover's less-than-heroic posturing during his capture, Karpis challenged the FBI on specific details surrounding his apprehension.

He questioned how Agent Connelly could have tackled him through the passenger side if Freddie Hunter had been occupying that seat. Then there was the rifle in the backseat, which Karpis had supposedly lunged towards.

His response: "What rifle? What backseat? We were in a 1936 Plymouth coupe that had no backseat. We had two rifles wrapped in a blanket to prevent damage to the sights, but they were locked away in the luggage compartment."

Karpis moved to Costa del Sol, Spain, in 1973 and had just finished chronicling his experiences in Alcatraz for Canadian author Robert Livesey when he died from an accidental sleeping pill overdose. He was 71. His follow-up book titled *On the Rock* was published in 1980.

Karpis' arrest not only marked the end of the era's public enemies, it also led to an intense FBI investigation into the political and police corruption in St. Paul, which accepted graft in exchange for protection. A citywide cleanup was enforced, and many of the high-level bosses such as Jack Peifer and Harry Sawyer were sentenced to lengthy jail terms. (Peifer's prison stay was shortened considerably when he committed suicide in his cell.)

Karpis endured hardships during his 25 years in Alcatraz, but even during his bleakest days, he never expressed regret at the path he had taken. Not when he recalled the abject poverty of some of the people he had met during his travels. In his memoirs, he wrote about a family he'd come across near Rush

Springs, Oklahoma. The father, mother and their three kids were living on land as parched and useless as desert sands, subsisting on a diet of salt pork and biscuits. Karpis bought the family a Victrola and fifty records just to put a little joy into their miserable existence.

Seeing the conditions that many were forced to live in during this period of American economic purgatory made Alvin Karpis glad he'd chosen to become a criminal.

CHAPTER SEVEN

Bonnie Parker (1910–1934) and Clyde Barrow (1909–1934)

"They wouldn't give up till they died."

–Bonnie Parker

DESPITE THE MOVIES, ballads and the couple's overall placement in popular culture, all of which have surrounded their legend with a gritty romanticism, the real Bonnie Parker and Clyde Barrow were nothing more than a pair of small-time criminals whose enduring myth is based more on fiction than fact.

Their career never reached the heights of their bandit counterparts, either in procedure or profits. Unlike John Dillinger, Alvin Karpis, or even the Barker boys, they were not bank-robbing masterminds. Neither were they Robin Hood desperadoes like Pretty Boy Floyd, nor misjudged innocents like Ma Barker.

They even differed from their closest rogue link, Baby Face Nelson, in that neither Bonnie nor Clyde possessed a contradiction in character. They were a simple pair who simply liked to steal and kill. During their violent odyssey, they were in 21 gun battles and murdered 11 peace officers and two civilians.

Their more passive pursuits included posing for gaudy photographs, which often displayed their vast arsenal. Clyde's guns were his passion. He cleaned them every night and even gave each a pet name. Both also possessed minimal artistic talent. Clyde enjoyed playing the saxophone, and Bonnie wrote poetry in which she tried to dispel their reputation through verse. But their primary bond was violence. They shared a love of killing, as if to compensate for the lack of intimacy in their relationship.

They were rumored to be a sexually perverse pair. Clyde was, if not homosexual, then certainly a man devoid of a normal sex drive. Bonnie, on the other hand, was reputed to be a nymphomaniac. With Clyde unable to satisfy her enormous sexual appetite, he often permitted a third partner to share their bed—usually their latest gang pickup.

While their criminal actions were initially applauded by rural folk forced from their homes and livelihoods by the pervading economic climate, public sympathy quickly shifted once the couple began preying on their own kind. Fellow criminals also shunned them. John Dillinger, for example, called Bonnie and Clyde "a couple of punks who give bank robbing a bad name." Even Pretty Boy Floyd kept his distance from the psychotic pair. In the final weeks of their lives, when the desperate duo expressed an interest in teaming up with Floyd, the Okie gangster bluntly instructed his family to ignore them if they ever came looking for him.

Floyd echoed Dillinger's sentiments: "Those two give us all a bad name."

Alvin Karpis was another who foresaw the trouble Bonnie and Clyde would bring to their profession. He first met the couple when he visited an associate living in Joplin, Missouri, who at the time was helping Bonnie and Clyde unload some Browning automatic rifles. Karpis' first impression of the pair was that they looked like sharecroppers. Both wore blank expressions (the girl, he recalled, had "awfully squinty eyes"), although their stares were piercing. As they silently left the

Bonnie Parker and Clyde Barrow: the most perverse pair of killers ever to terrorize the Southwest

house after their unsuccessful transaction, Karpis remembered thinking that wherever Bonnie and Clyde went, trouble was sure to follow.

Karpis' thoughts proved prophetic. Bad times did indeed accompany the pair as they whipped up dust and blood across five southwestern states. Bonnie and Clyde terrorized gas stations, grocery stores, luncheonettes and small-town banks throughout Texas, Oklahoma, Missouri, Louisiana and

New Mexico. Their crime spree lasted just two years, their biggest haul reported to be a mere $3600. Yet their penchant for violence placed them at the forefront of the era's most wanted criminals.

Neither had the appearance of a killer. Both possessed youthful, rather pleasant features. Bonnie was an attractive, golden-haired girl with bright blue eyes, a light, freckled complexion and a pouty mouth. Clyde had a face that was equally as delicate, almost choirboy innocent, which complemented his apparent effeminate nature.

Both were slight of build. Bonnie stood 4'11" and weighed 90 pounds. Clyde was just under 5'7", weighing in at 130 pounds. But like other diminutive desperadoes (Baby Face Nelson and the Barkers), they compensated for their short stature by becoming proficient with firearms. Clyde in particular was an expert marksman, especially if his target was the "laws."

Clyde Chestnut Barrow entered the world on March 24, 1909, in Teleco, Texas. He was the fifth of eight children born to Henry and Cumie Barrow, poor sharecroppers who raised their family in a rundown clapboard farmhouse. As a young boy, Clyde was adventurous and showed little fear both in his game playing and in his frequent wanderings from home. Even at an early age, Clyde began exhibiting sadistic tendencies, mostly directed at birds, stray pets and barnyard animals. One of his favorite pastimes was stealing chickens from neighboring farms for cockfighting.

He had little interest in education and dropped out of school after the sixth grade, choosing instead to follow the example set by older brother Melvin Ivan Barrow (better known as Buck), a born hellion whose criminal pursuits had progressed from selling stolen turkeys to stealing cars.

Ironically, Clyde's own larcenous leanings began with his love of music. When his parents were unable to buy Clyde the saxophone he so desperately wanted, he went out and stole one, demonstrating early on the effect poverty can have in breeding a criminal mind. From that moment on, he simply took anything he wanted. But his juvenile crime spree came to an abrupt halt when, at age 10, the police collared him and sent him to the Harris County School for Boys, where he was labeled "an incorrigible truant, thief and runaway."

When Clyde was released from reform school in his early teens, he followed his family to Dallas where Henry ran a combination gas station/grocery store. The Barrow clan's fortunes improved slightly, but Clyde could not seem to stay out of trouble. He hooked up with the "Root Square Gang," a group of restless, rebellious youths who specialized in burglaries, car theft and street muggings. Clyde's budding criminal career received further encouragement from brother Buck, who took him along on several small-time holdups in the Dallas area. Buck saw a lot of potential in his kid brother, who maintained the same fearless demeanor he had shown as a child. By the time Clyde reached his early twenties, he had become a habitual criminal with no desire to pursue any other life.

In October 1929, Clyde, Buck and two other men stole a car and drove into the town of Denton where they broke into a garage and carried out the safe. Clyde was behind the wheel as they made their getaway, but his driving was reckless, attracting the attention of local police, who gave chase. Clyde's attempts to elude his pursuers caused him to momentarily spin out of control, slamming the car into a curb and snapping both axles. Clyde was thrown from the car. He scrambled to his feet and started running, leaving the dazed Buck behind. As Buck recovered, he pulled his pistol and fired at the advancing patrolmen, who drew their own weapons.

Buck received a flesh wound in the exchange before being overcome and taken into custody along with one of his crew.

For his part in the Denton robbery, Buck Barrow was sentenced to five years in the state penitentiary at Huntsville. He took the full rap, failing to implicate either his brother or the other accomplice who had gotten away. Clyde felt guilty about running out on Buck, but he was glad to be free. He decided to lay low for a while.

Bonnie Parker had been chorin' as a waitress prior to meeting Clyde Barrow. In her own words, she was "bored crapless" and yearned for excitement. She was 19 years old and married, although her husband, Roy Thornton, was serving a five-year stretch for robbery.

Bonnie was born in Rowena, Texas, on October 1, 1910. Her station in life was slightly better than Clyde's. Her father Henry was employed as a bricklayer and had the means to at least provide the basics for Bonnie, older brother Hubert (nicknamed Buster) and baby sister Billie. But when Henry died in 1914, his widow Emma was forced to move the family to Cement City, where they lived with her mother.

Bonnie was a bright student with a particular flair for artistic expression, displayed most prominently in her creative writing. She was attractive and popular, but she also had a violent temper that could be unleashed at the slightest provocation.

At Cement City High School, she began dating Roy Thornton, who was two years her senior. Her passion for Thornton was so great that, over her mother's objections, she married him the following year when she turned 16.

Shortly thereafter, circumstances forced the couple to move in with Emma Parker, an arrangement that Thornton resented. In his frustration, he disappeared for long periods, getting drunk and dabbling in petty crime. Finally, after Bonnie threw him out of the house for his continued absences,

Roy was arrested for a robbery at Red Oak and sentenced to a five-year jail term.

Bonnie found work as a cafe waitress, but lost her job during the early months of the Depression. She went to stay with a friend in West Dallas and there met Clyde Barrow, who happened to drop by one day. Bonnie was immediately attracted to Clyde, in whom she discerned a likeness of spirit.

Despite his questionable sexual preferences, Clyde wasn't averse to Bonnie's affections. He'd had two previous relationships, neither of which had been successful. But Bonnie was persistent, and Clyde liked her spunk. Before long, the two were living together.

Even if they'd enjoyed a traditional romance, their relationship was tainted from the start. First, Clyde was picked up for the garage robbery in Denton, although he was later released for insufficient evidence. Then, Waco authorities arrested him on outstanding warrants including auto theft and burglary. Bonnie must have known that Clyde was no innocent, but perhaps she couldn't have imagined losing a second beau to prison.

Clyde was sentenced to two years in the Waco jail. However, on March 11, 1930, nine days after he began serving time, Bonnie visited Clyde with a .38 Colt revolver taped to her thigh. She secretly passed it through the bars to him, and that night, Clyde and two other convicts forced their way out of the jail at gunpoint. They stole a car and high-tailed it to Abilene.

Clyde had hoped to meet up with Buck on learning that his brother had also escaped from jail just four days earlier (though with less dramatic flair—Buck simply walked off the prison farm, where he had been given certain privileges for being a model prisoner). But the brothers' reunion would have to wait. Buck's first priority was to marry Blanche Caldwell, a girl he'd been seeing prior to his imprisonment.

Then, only a week after his escape, Clyde was recaptured in Middleton, Ohio, where he and his two accomplices held up a dry-cleaning firm and the offices of the Baltimore and Ohio Railroad. He returned to the Waco jail, and on April 21, 1930, he was transferred to Eastham Prison Farm Number 2 in Huntsville to begin a 14-year sentence. Reportedly, Bonnie "cried constantly" at his conviction.

Eastham (also known as "The Walls" and "The Burning Hell") was an unbearable experience even for an incorrigible man like Clyde Barrow (Prisoner #63527). He spent long days laboring in the fields under a blazing September sun only to sit down to improperly cooked meals, often prepared from spoiled foodstuffs. He was beaten with a leather strap for the slightest infraction of prison rules, or he was made to sit on a pickle barrel mounted atop a sawhorse and suffer the intense heat from the sun until he collapsed from exhaustion. Also, both guards and inmates apparently made homosexual advances towards the boyish-looking Clyde.

Desperate to obtain a transfer, he persuaded a fellow convict on work detail to miss a swing with his axe and chop off two of his toes. The man complied, but Clyde's deliberate mutilation proved unnecessary. While recovering in the prison hospital, he got word that he had been granted parole after his mother Cumie appeared before Texas Governor Ross Sterling and pleaded for his release. Clyde limped out of the prison gates on crutches on February 2, 1932, 20 months after he'd first arrived.

He swore never to see the inside of another jail, vowing: "I'll die first." It was a promise he kept.

Clyde reunited with Bonnie, but was disappointed to learn that brother Buck, at Blanche's urging, had voluntarily returned to prison to serve out his time in the hope of making a fresh start. Clyde realized that he, too, had the opportunity to go straight, if that was what he wanted. But honest work was not for him. He was itching to put into practical application the bank-robbing education he had received during his stint at Eastham.

Bonnie saw that Clyde was of no mind to reform, and either because of her devotion to him, or perhaps because of her own need to escape a stifling environment, she chose to accompany him on his lawless travels. Bonnie explained her leaving to her mother simply by saying that she had found a job in Houston demonstrating cosmetic products.

In March 1932, Bonnie Parker and Clyde Barrow, in the company of Eastham alumni Raymond Hamilton and Ralph Fults, drove into Kaufman, Texas. Bonnie got an early taste of what she was in for when the gang held up the local hardware store. She acted as a nervous lookout while the three men looted the cash register. Suddenly, the burglar alarm sounded, and the bandits beat a hasty retreat, speeding off in their stolen car with the police in pursuit. While negotiating the unfamiliar back roads, Clyde overrode a curve and crashed the car into a tree. He grabbed Bonnie and led her to an empty building, where he told her to wait for him until he found another car. Bonnie did as she was told, but when Clyde was slow in returning, she grew impatient and decided to leave on her own. The police spotted her walking along a dirt road in her bare feet and picked her up on suspicion of complicity in the robbery.

Unaware of Bonnie's predicament and unable to find a car to steal, Clyde, Hamilton and Fults continued to trek through the night. Fults parted company with the others and was later arrested by police.

Three days following Bonnie's arrest and lockup in the Kaufman jail, Clyde was short of cash, so he robbed the Sims Oil Company in Dallas. Then, shortly after midnight on April 27, he and Ray Hamilton arrived in Hillsboro and shot to death 61-year-old jewelry store owner John Bucher for a small amount of cash and diamond rings valued at $2500. Clyde Barrow had committed his first murder. There was no turning back.

On June 17, Bonnie Parker, after languishing in a jail cell at Kaufman, Texas, for three months, appeared before the grand jury at Kaufman. The case against her was not strong, and after tearfully convincing the jury of her contrition, she was released and went home to her mother.

On August 5, after crossing into Oklahoma, Clyde, Ray Hamilton and Hamilton's pal Everett Milligan were sitting in their car drinking bootleg whiskey while watching a barn dance just outside Atoka. Sheriff C.G. Maxwell and Undersheriff Eugene Moore grew suspicious of the trio and walked towards their vehicle. As Maxwell leaned inside the open window to speak, Clyde casually withdrew his gun and fired. Maxwell dropped. Clyde then turned his gun on Moore. Eugene Moore died of a bullet to the heart.

The gunshots shattered the quiet summer night, interrupting the festivities. As patrons began to advance on the outlaws, Clyde slammed the car into gear and gunned the engine to 70 miles per hour, hurtling forward across the grass, scattering the would-be heroes and leaving behind the screams of the dancers and the popping gunfire directed at them from the wounded sheriff.

Bonnie returned briefly to waitressing but became bored and restless, and most of all, missed Clyde. She didn't stay long either at home with her mother or at the cafe. On August 12, Clyde came to get her, and Bonnie Parker became his partner-in-crime for the next 21 months.

The timing couldn't have been worse. The authorities picked up Everett Milligan, and he talked freely about the Atoka slaying of Eugene Moore. State Governor Ross Sterling, who had signed Clyde's release from Eastham, offered a $250 reward for Clyde Barrow's capture.

Ray Hamilton hadn't yet been identified as part of the gang. Although shorter even than Clyde, Hamilton had a hair-trigger temper and possessed a sadistic streak that complemented Clyde Barrow's own crazy nature. Hamilton was also useful to Clyde in another way. He was the first to participate in the strange three-way sleeping arrangements of Bonnie and Clyde. But to Clyde Barrow sexual pleasures weren't as exciting or as fulfilling as pulling off a successful robbery. He'd often stay awake late into the night planning and strategizing the gang's next heist, completely oblivious to the "activities" going on in the bedroom.

In September 1932, Clyde and Ray raided the National Guard Armory at Fort Worth, escaping with a good portion of its arsenal. Equipped with professional weapons and well supplied with ammunition, the gang returned to banditry and held up the Abilene State Bank. Their take was a modest $1400.

While their scores were unimpressive, their reputation with the law was growing. Shortly after hitting Abilene, they narrowly escaped a police blockade on the bridge spanning the Colorado River. Only Clyde's much-improved driving skills saved them from speeding into a potential ambush.

But Ray Hamilton needed a breather, so he departed the gang to visit his father in Michigan. One night Ray drank too much and talked too much. He was arrested and extradited to Texas, where he was tried and sentenced to 263 years in the penitentiary at Huntsville.

But being minus a partner didn't slow Bonnie and Clyde's momentum. Next, they hit a grocery store in Sherman, Texas, where Clyde added another notch to his gun by firing six rounds from his .45 into butcher Howard Hall, who lunged at Clyde with a meat cleaver and missed. The man died hours later, all for cash totaling $50.

Clyde never expressed remorse at his killings, but he did try to justify them. In Howard Hall's case, Clyde felt he could rightly claim self-defense. Still, he had no reservations about settling disputes with the discharge of his gun.

On November 14, while Bonnie sat outside in the car with the engine running, Clyde walked into the Oranogo, Missouri, state bank and pulled off his first solo bank robbery for a grand total of $115. It was time to take on a new recruit, both for professional and personal reasons. In December, they found a suitable candidate in 16-year-old William Daniel (W.D.) Jones, a gas station attendant and aspiring thief, who was eager, impressionable and in awe of the criminal adventures of Clyde Barrow.

But W.D.'s "thrill ride" soon became a nightmare of violence and alleged physical and sexual abuse, which he was forced to endure for 18 months. Clyde decided to test his apprentice on Christmas Day, 1932, when he ordered him to steal a car belonging to salesman Doyle Johnson. Johnson walked outside, saw what was happening and rushed towards Jones. That was when Clyde stepped forward, sending a single bullet from his automatic into Doyle's neck. Although he had not fired the fatal shot, W.D. Jones had received his blood initiation into the Barrow Gang.

Later, according to Jones' 28-page confession, the months that followed included machine-gun bank robberies, random killings and sexual ravages by both Bonnie and Clyde. When he was not needed to satisfy their individual sexual urges, he claimed he was tied up with chains so he couldn't escape. Following his capture, he literally trembled as he begged authorities to keep him safe from sadistic retribution at the hands of Bonnie and Clyde.

It was a happy day for Clyde when, on March 20, 1933, Buck Barrow walked from prison a free man. Taking a cue from her mother-in-law, Blanche Barrow had gone before the Texas governor and employed the same tactics to obtain the release of her husband.

Miriam "Ma" Ferguson, who was sympathetic and generous in handing out pardons, had replaced Governor Sterling, who had issued the cash reward for Clyde. Blanche's tearful plea of how she had to raise three children on her own (with another on the way) so softened the governor's heart that she signed Buck Barrow's release papers. Two days later he walked through the gates of Huntsville. Sadly, the kind-hearted Ma Ferguson would live to regret her decision.

While in prison, one of Buck's duties had been to clean up the death house following an execution, and while sweeping up bunches of burned hair, he often envisioned Clyde strapped to the electric chair. He bemoaned the fact that he was not there to set his younger brother straight. Maybe his concerns while locked behind bars were genuine, but once free, Buck's promise to guide brother Clyde took on another direction.

Clyde and Buck eventually got together on a quiet back road in Joplin, where they whooped it up and made great plans for their future. Blanche wasn't particularly happy about the brothers' criminal partnership, but her love for Buck overrode her concerns, and she decided to stick by him whatever the outcome.*

Rough days were ahead. Throughout March and April, the gang robbed a jewelry store in Neosho, Missouri, replenished their arsenal in Springfield and then swept into Kansas City to hold up a loan office. Bloodshed continued when, after a two-week hiatus, police raided their Joplin hideout. A wild gun battle ensued, during which Constable Wes Harryman and Detective Harry L. McGuiness were killed. Both Clyde and W.D. Jones received minor wounds in the shootout, but the gang escaped, with Clyde taking the wheel and then driving

---

*Buck and Blanche stayed near Dallas until after Blanche gave birth, then the couple took to the road, leaving their four children behind.

nearly 400 miles across Oklahoma into Texas. Bonnie had proven her mettle during the gunfight, when she suddenly appeared at the second-story window firing an automatic rifle right back at the law.

Clyde was proud to bursting and later said: "That Bonnie is sure full of piss and vinegar."

The Joplin shootout brought further notoriety to the names Bonnie and Clyde, although Clyde was sometimes dubbed the "Texas Rattlesnake" and Bonnie "Suicide Sal."

Bonnie's nickname was most likely inspired by a poem she wrote, later found by the police, called *The Story of Suicide Sal*. At a later date, she penned another lengthy verse entitled *The Story of Bonnie and Clyde*. The latter poem was poor biography but ultimately proved prophetic.

> *You have heard the story of Jesse James,*
> *Of how he lived and died.*
> *If you're still in need of something to read,*
> *Here's the story of Bonnie and Clyde.*
>
> *Now Bonnie and Clyde are the Barrow gang,*
> *I'm sure you all have read*
> *How they rob and steal,*
> *And how those who squeal,*
> *Are usually found dying or dead.*
>
> *There's lots of untruths to these write-ups,*
> *They're not so ruthless as that;*
> *Their nature is raw, they hate all the laws,*
> *The stool pigeons, spotters and rats.*
>
> *They call them cold-blooded killers,*
> *They say they are heartless and mean;*
> *But I say this with pride,*

That I once knew Clyde
When he was honest and upright and clean.

But the laws fooled around,
Kept taking him down
And locking him up in a cell,
Till he said to me,
"I'll never be free,
So I'll meet a few of them in hell."

The road was so dimly lighted,
There were no highway signs to guide,
But they made up their minds
If all roads were blind,
They wouldn't give up till they died.

The road gets dimmer and dimmer,
Sometimes you can hardly see,
But it's fight, man to man,
And do all you can,
For they know they can never be free.

From heartbreak some people have suffered,
From weariness some people have died,
But take it all in all,
Our troubles are small
Till we get like Bonnie and Clyde.

If a policeman is killed in Dallas,
And they have no clues to guide,
If they can't find a fiend,
They just wipe their slate clean
And hang it on Bonnie and Clyde.

> *There's two crimes committed in America*
> *Not accredited to the Barrow mob;*
> *They had no hand*
> *In the kidnap demand,*
> *Nor the Kansas City depot job.*

Bonnie's protests of unfair persecution brought the Barrow Gang no sympathy as the outlaws went right on with their lawless ventures and damn the consequences. In 1933, they robbed three banks: the Lucerne State Bank in Indiana of $300, the Alma State Bank in Texas and then hit one of their biggest paydays when they held up the First State Bank of Okabena on May 16 and drove away with $2500.

In early June, Clyde, Bonnie and W.D. Jones, were speeding across Texas towards the Oklahoma border to rendezvous with Buck and Blanche, when Clyde noticed almost at the last moment that the bridge he was approaching was closed for repairs. He swerved, and the car crashed down a steep embankment. Clyde and Jones were thrown clear, but Bonnie was trapped inside as the car exploded into flames.

Clyde rushed towards the car and struggled to free her from the inferno. Bonnie's agony was such that she pleaded with him just to shoot her. Fortunately, two farmers who were nearby rushed to the scene and helped pull Bonnie from the car. They carried her to a nearby farmhouse, where the wife of one of the men tended to her burn injuries as best she could. It was clear that the girl needed proper medical attention, but when Clyde adamantly refused their offer to call an ambulance, the other farmer became suspicious and snuck away to call the local police.

A little later, two lawmen crept up to the house, only to be greeted by the rifle-wielding Clyde and W.D. Jones. The outlaws promptly handcuffed the pair, took them hostage and commandeered their car in order to make their rendezvous with Buck and Blanche. It has been speculated that the only reason Sheriff Dick Corey and Wellington City Marshall Paul Hardy were spared by the cop-hating Clyde is because they showed genuine concern for Bonnie.

Buck and Blanche were horrified at the severity of Bonnie's burns, which scarred and blistered the lower part of her face, both shoulders and the whole of her right leg. So with Clyde refusing to leave Bonnie's bedside, Buck and W.D. had to replenish the gang's cash supply.

On June 23, they drove into Fayetteville, Texas, and robbed a Piggly Wiggly store. Marshall Henry D. Humphrey tried to halt their getaway, and the bandits shot him dead. Buck and W.D. then sped away in the murdered lawman's car. Once again the heat was on, and the outlaws were forced to take it on the run while Bonnie continued to endure the pain of her injuries.

Bonnie's brush with death and the knowledge of the shoot-to-kill bounty on their heads prompted her to pen a note to her mother. She wrote: "When they kill us Mama, bring me home. Please don't let them lay me out in a funeral parlor."

The five criminals were never in one place for long, spending most of their waking hours behind the wheel of a car, usually a stolen vehicle to which the gang would affix any of hundreds of state license plates they had collected in order to throw police off their trail. But their fugitive lifestyle was rapidly wearing thin, particularly for Blanche, who was often given to uncontrollable screaming fits.

Unlike John Dillinger, the Barker-Karpis Gang or even Baby Face Nelson, who could pay for high-cost protection in such Midwest cities as St. Paul, where they could enjoy plush hotel accommodations and fine dining privileges, Bonnie and Clyde usually slept by campfires, subsisting on coffee and peanut butter and jelly sandwiches.

When they could afford less rustic accommodations, they would either pull into remote tourist camps or fishing grounds.

But such respites were usually brief. The proprietor quickly became suspicious and notified the police, who would wait until nightfall before moving in to investigate.

A newsboy once said to his buddy:
I wish old Clyde would get jumped;
In these awful hard times
We'd make a few dimes
If five or six cops would get bumped.

The police haven't got the report yet,
But Clyde called me up today;
He said, "Don't start any fights—
We aren't working nights—
We're joining the NRA.

From Irving to West Dallas viaduct
Is known as the Great Divide,
Where the women are kin,
And the men are men,
And they won't stool on Bonnie and Clyde.

If they try to act like citizens,
And rent them a nice little flat,
About the third night they are invited to fight
By a submachine gun rat-tat-tat.

The Barrow Gang drove to the Red Crown Tavern six miles outside of Platte City, Missouri, where they hoped to enjoy a few days' rest. But the odd comings and goings of the group aroused the suspicions of hotel owner Emmett Breen, who called the local police.

Suspecting that they might be dealing with the Barrow Gang, Sheriff Coffey quickly assembled a posse. The special squad moved onto the campgrounds at 11:00 PM accompanied by an armored car. Each of the men was issued a steel shield for protection from the gangsters.

Sheriff Coffey knocked on the door of Buck and Blanche's cottage, announcing who he was and ordering them to come out. Moments later, Clyde swung open the garage door, simultaneously tugging the trigger of his Browning automatic rifle. Sheriff Coffey tried to find cover. Despite the shield's protection, one of Clyde's bullets hit the lawman in the neck.

The posse returned fire, their relentless shower of bullets shattering windows and blasting apart the wood framing of the cottage. The outlaws focused much of their firepower on the formidable armored car. A deputy stationed inside took a slug in the leg.

Buck used a mattress from the bed for cover and rushed from his cabin spraying hot lead. He kept firing until Blanche got safely to their car, already revving in the garage. Then, a well-aimed police bullet plowed into his temple, and he fell to the ground with his gun still blazing.

Suddenly, the Ford V8 rocketed out of the garage, with Clyde at the wheel and W.D. on the running board firing a machine gun. They collected Buck who, although conscious, had blood flowing from a head wound, and roared off down a dark country road. The police continued firing, their barrage of bullets blasting out the car windows. A stray shard of glass sliced into Blanche's face, dousing her eyes with blood.

When they were many miles away, Clyde drove into a field so the gang could take stock of their injuries. Sheriff Coffey, who paid no heed to his own wound, rushed to organize a search party. Surveying the bloodied battleground where the outlaws had made their stand, it appeared to Sheriff Coffey and his deputies that they had gotten in a few good licks at the Barrow Gang.

Miraculously, no lawmen were seriously wounded in the shootout, but Buck Barrow was another story. The gunshot to his temple was serious, and unless he received immediate medical attention, he wouldn't survive. Clyde had a dilemma. If they took Buck to a hospital and he recovered, he would be arrested, tried and probably executed. Clyde made the difficult decision just to keep Buck comfortable and let him die in his own time.

He knew he'd made the right choice (against Blanche's objections) when his brother regained consciousness long enough to say to his weeping wife, "We won't give up, honey. We keep on driving."

Which they did—on into Iowa. Clyde located a quiet wooded area in Dexter where Buck could die peacefully. No such luck. On the morning of July 24, as the women prepared breakfast at their campsite, police officers from Des Moines, National Guardsmen and even eager farmers had formed their own posse and closed in on the gang.

It was Bonnie who first spotted their movement through the trees, and she called out a familiar warning: "It's the law!"

The 100-man team opened fire. Clyde and W.D. quickly collected weapons and shot back. They dashed towards their two cars. As Blanche helped Buck to his feet, a bullet slammed into his back, thrusting him forward. Clyde was already behind the wheel of his car, but a bullet clipped his arm. As the car spun around, it crashed into a tree stump, so he jumped out and ran towards the second vehicle. But the posse anticipated his move and redirected their fire, blasting away at the car, puncturing the tires, shattering the windows and piercing the gas tank.

The outlaws' only hope was to escape on foot into the surrounding woodlands. But they'd never get far with Buck, and Clyde refused to leave his brother behind. Buck, however, knew that the game was over. He struggled to his feet while firing careless rounds from his automatic. The posse responded by blowing five more holes into him.

Clyde could do nothing more but rush into the woods alongside Bonnie and W.D., twisting and ducking as the bullets whizzed past them. Blanche stayed behind, cradling her husband's head in her lap as she screamed at the posse to stop their firing.

"Don't shoot anymore! You've already killed him!"

She fought against the men who tried to pull her from Buck's crouched, blood-soaked form, her voice pitifully childlike as she cried, "Don't die, Daddy! Please, Daddy, don't die!"

Five days later, Buck Barrow did exactly that.

Clyde suffered pangs of conscience at once again deserting his brother, as he had done when they'd robbed the gas station in Denton an eternity ago. And Buck replayed his protective big brother role by swearing with his dying breath that it was he and not Clyde who had killed Sheriff Humphrey in Fayetteville.

Blanche's role in the Barrow Gang landed her 10 years in the Women's Prison at Jefferson City. During the trial, Platte City officials took extra precautions to guard the courthouse, thinking that Clyde might try to rescue his neurotic sister-in-law.

The three survivors of the Barrow Gang continued with "pocket-money" stickups until the 17-year-old W.D. Jones willingly surrendered himself to the authorities on November 15, 1933, in Houston. He immediately used the opportunity to reveal the whole story of his "18 months of hell" with Bonnie and Clyde. His graphic depictions were regarded as either a sincere confession or a desperate attempt to evoke public sympathy.

With Buck dead, W.D. in custody and Bonnie still suffering from her burn injuries, Clyde needed to rebuild his gang. He wanted seasoned, dependable professionals. He heard that his old partner Ray Hamilton was planning to bust out of the

Eastham prison farm. Clyde immediately sent word through a contact that he would help Ray in his escape.

The break was set for January 16, 1934, during outdoor work detail. Secretly supplied with .45 automatics, Hamilton and a convict named Joe Palmer fatally wounded guard Major Crowson and then, with 21-year-old Henry Methvin, rushed into the early morning fog towards the waiting Barrow car.

The fugitives barely had time to catch their breath before they went to work. Four days following the break, the gang hit a bank in Lancaster, Texas. Their take was estimated at between $2400 and $6700, although the amount was likely closer to the lower figure.

While their scores were embarrassingly small compared to what Dillinger and other bank robbers were raking in, the Barrow Gang had so terrorized the Southwest that the sheriff of Dallas County appealed to State Governor Miriam Ferguson to bring back into active duty legendary Texas Ranger Frank Hamer.

Fifty-year-old Hamer had resigned from law enforcement two years earlier after a spectacular career of captures and outlaw shootouts. He was a man of single-minded purpose who rarely failed to bring in his man. Few doubted that Frank Hamer could end the bloody reign of Bonnie and Clyde.

An old acquaintance of Bonnie's during her days as a waitress, Deputy Sheriff Ted Hinton, also joined in the hunt following the November 8 robbery of the McMurray Oil Refinery payroll office. Hinton found it difficult to believe that the petite, sweet-faced girl he used to admire from afar had become one of the country's most wanted criminals. (As a macabre side note: Hinton later recalled both Bonnie and Clyde's families visiting a funeral home during the height of the couple's crime spree to select their caskets.)

The Barrow Gang hit again on February 19, 1934, lifting weapons and ammunition from the National Guard Armory at Ranger, Texas, and putting them to use robbing the bank in Lancaster.

At some point a falling out occurred between Ray and Clyde. The two parted company, but such was Clyde's bitterness towards Hamilton that he plotted an ambush at an old meeting grounds on Easter Sunday, April 1. Hamilton didn't show up to collect his promised share of the Lancaster bank loot, but motorcycle patrolmen E.G. Wheeler and H.D. Murphy did. According to a witness, Clyde gunned down the two officers, and then a young woman ran over to one of the men and fired several more shots into his body.

On April 25, Hamilton meekly surrendered to police who'd cornered him on the main highway leading into Oklahoma. As he raised his hands in the air, he confessed his identity and added, "I don't intend to give you no trouble. I'm fresh out of ammunition, money, whiskey and women. Let's just go to jail." (On May 10, 1935, both Raymond Hamilton and Joe Palmer sat in the electric chair at the Huntsville penitentiary for the murder of prison guard Major Crowson.)

Sensing that their own end was near, Bonnie and Clyde arranged a meeting with their folks on a rural road near Dallas on May 10. The youthful Henry Methvin listened as Bonnie said her final goodbyes to her mother. It was then that he fully understood the reality of their situation. Methvin knew his own case was desperate, especially since Clyde had made him an accessory to the murders of the two motorcycle cops.

Meanwhile, Frank Hamer, learning of the Barrow/Parker family reunion, correctly assumed that Henry Methvin would next try to visit his father Irvin, who lived in Arcadia, Louisiana. The Methvin farm was a perfect stopover for the gang since it was isolated and accessible only by one narrow dirt road. But whether Irvin Methvin made a deal with Hamer to set up Bonnie and Clyde in exchange for leniency for his son has never really been ascertained. But that is most likely

Bonnie and Clyde's bullet-riddled death car, a testament to the posse's decision not to take them alive, enjoyed an unusual post-mortem history. A showman obtained the vehicle and displayed it in various small Texas towns, where he spoke none too kindly of the cowardly way Bonnie and Clyde met their end. Frank Hamer and Manny Gault heard these comments and became outraged at the accusations. Hamer took to the floor, physically slapping the car's owner across the room. The car (and custom-built substitutes) was displayed at carnivals in the U.S. and Canada along with actual and mock film footage showing Bonnie and Clyde's killing. Since 2000, the death car has been a tourist attraction at the Primm Valley Resort and Casino, 40 miles south of Las Vegas.

what happened because Henry was not with the pair on their drive back to the Methvin farm that fateful day, apparently having deserted Bonnie and Clyde during a shopping trip into Shreveport.

It is known that Hamer, together with Ted Hinton, P.M. Oakley, B.M. Gault, Bob Alcorn and Henderson Jordan, mapped out the site and decided on a location near Gibland to wait in ambush for Bonnie and Clyde. There was never any question about their being taken alive. Past attempts to capture the outlaw couple had always resulted in fatal shootouts. This time, Hamer wanted to ensure that the gunplay would be one-sided.

For three days, the six-man posse secured themselves among the trees and dense bushes that bordered the road leading to the Methvin farmhouse. Then, at approximately 9:15 on the morning of May 23, 1934, they spotted a tan-colored Ford coupe rolling towards them down the dusty back road.

The posse, dirty and bewhiskered, tired and edgy from their lengthy vigil, wiped the fatigue from their eyes and readied their weapons, which included rifles, shotguns, machine guns and a Browning automatic rifle.

Once the men had the car's occupants squarely in their gun sights, Captain Hamer gave the order to open fire. The early morning quiet was instantly shattered. For more than a minute, a steady barrage of gunfire ripped into the vehicle. The coupe resembled a sieve as it slowed and veered lazily into a ditch.

Bonnie and Clyde were killed instantly, their bodies torn apart by the steel-jacketed bullets dispensed by the officers' high-powered weaponry. The force of these bullets was so great that many of the shells slammed through Clyde and also through Bonnie in their dance of death, then exited out the passenger door. A total of 184 bullets were fired at the car.

Despite Bonnie's poetic prediction, she and Clyde were not buried side by side. Clyde rests next to his brother Buck.

⁓ᦙᏟᦙ⁓

Clyde was hit 54 times, his left hand severed at the wrist. Bonnie's body, which had slumped against Clyde's in a final embrace, actually sustained more bullet wounds due to the crossfire of the ambush.

It didn't take long for the curious to descend on the death scene. Photographs and even a motion picture record were taken just moments following the ambush. Scavengers tried to remove pieces of clothing and other "souvenirs" from the bodies, with one man even trying to sever Clyde's ear as a gruesome memento.

Had Bonnie and Clyde been given the chance to shoot it out, the outcome might have been different. An inventory of their car revealed a small arsenal, including two sawed-off shotguns, two machine rifles, 10 automatic pistols and 1500 rounds of ammunition.

An examination of their bodies at the scene showed that Clyde Barrow died in his stocking feet while Bonnie wore a flowered hat and had a new permanent wave. Resting in her lifeless hand was not a pistol, but a half-eaten sandwich.

The fact that they met their end while indulging in simple pleasures perhaps adds a human quality to the murderous lives of Bonnie Parker and Clyde Barrow. Yet it does not diminish the bloody legacy with which both achieved their dubious immortality.

> *They don't think they're too smart or desperate,*
> *They know that the law always wins;*
> *They've been shot at before, but they do not ignore*
> *That death is the wages of sin.*

> *Some day they will go down together,*
> *And they will bury them side by side,*
> *To a few it means grief,*
> *To the law it's relief,*
> *But it's death to Bonnie and Clyde.*

–Bonnie Parker

CHAPTER EIGHT

Francis "Two Gun" Crowley
(1911–1931)

"You sons 'o bitches. Give my love to Mother."
–The final words of Francis "Two Gun" Crowley

IN A WAY IT WAS IRONIC. Nineteen-year-old baby-faced killer, Francis "Two Gun" Crowley, being put to death the same year 31-year-old James Cagney exploded onto movie screens as the ruthless Tom Powers in *The Public Enemy*. Crowley had probably never even heard of Cagney, who was destined to become the preeminent purveyor of early cinematic violence. Yet it was almost certainly Two Gun Crowley's own brief and bloody career that gave the impetus for Cagney's colorful parade of tough-guy characters. It's easy to imagine Warner Brothers screenwriters, always on the lookout for potent headline material, using Crowley's manic exploits as inspiration for gangster scripts specially tailored for Cagney. Beyond their diminutive statures and shared Irish heritage, they both possessed hair-trigger tempers (although Cagney's flare-ups were confined to movie sets, unless his target was Jack L. Warner). Cagney's greatest gangster movies depicted him as an amoral, antisocial, cop-hating murderer whose only hint of decency was his love for his mother.

Consider Cagney's Academy Award-nominated role in the 1938 film *Angels with Dirty Faces*. The actor plays a slum kid turned big-shot racketeer who is coined "Two Gun" Rocky Sullivan by the newspapers. His character shares Crowley's fate: he goes to the chair, but not before shooting it out with the cops in a prolonged gun battle that ends only when Rocky is forced out of his hideout by tear gas.

Then there is the role in which Cagney gives what many still consider his most memorable hoodlum performance as Cody Jarrett in *White Heat*. Whether or not he knew it at the time, the 49-year-old actor captured perfectly both the psychopathic savagery and perverted sensitivity of a long-dead and nearly forgotten teenage outlaw.

James Cagney wasn't the only movie tough guy to play roles influenced by Two Gun Crowley. In 1940, John Garfield starred as Tommy Gordon in *Castle on the Hudson*, another Warner Brothers crime drama, based on the book *20,000 Years in Sing Sing* by Warden Lewis Lawes. Lawes, regarded as one the country's leading penologists, got to know and understand Crowley (as much as anyone could) during the criminal's stay on death row. He offered insight into Crowley's sympathetic qualities as well as his swaggering bravado when fashioning the title character for his story.

Crowley believed and reveled in his own press, but he wasn't content to sit back and let eager journalists feed the public lies and half-truths. Crowley was determined to initiate his own publicity and do whatever it took to perpetuate his gangster image.

For Two Gun Crowley, that wasn't a difficult chore. Before he turned 20, he referred to himself as "the toughest man in New York," and he was ready to take on any and all who would challenge his boast. His efforts to live up to his claim culminated in New York's most famous cops-and-robbers gun battle, where a sneering, defiant Crowley shot it out with more than 300 police officers in what became known as "The Siege of W. 90th Street."

Some believe that a person's path in life is predetermined. That greatness or infamy is stamped upon an individual from the moment of birth. Perhaps that was the case with Francis Crowley, who was born into miserable, fatherless surroundings on Halloween, 1911. His mother, who was of German descent and toiled as a housekeeper, realized that she would not be able to provide for her son, and she had the infant Francis placed in a foster home.

The boy left school after the third grade and remained almost illiterate throughout his life. Police later speculated that he may even have been mildly retarded. Francis' primary education was a reflection of his tough New York neighborhood. While his physical weakness and timid nature made him a non-entity among the local street toughs, he fueled his imagination by devouring dime-store crime and detective magazines. At an early age, Francis secretly settled on the path he would follow in life.

He loved the early gangster movies and always cheered on the bad guy, particularly enjoying the scenes where a policeman was killed onscreen. He harbored a deep-rooted hatred of police ever since learning from his foster mother that his biological grandfather, a respected police captain, had been a cold and cruel man towards his family.

For some reason, his contempt for the law remained firm in Francis' mind. He would often lose himself in violent fantasies where he single-handedly struck back at the police, whom he always envisioned as the image of his grandfather.

Despite his twisted imagination, Francis' boyhood was uneventful. At age 12, he was put to work in a factory, where he labored long hours at menial tasks. When he received his weekly pay envelope, he dutifully turned it over to his foster mother, whom he had come to love and regard as his natural parent. She later remembered Francis as a quiet boy, who chose to be alone a lot. But she maintained that he'd never displayed any criminal or violent behavior. To all outward appearances, Francis Crowley was a hard-working boy devoted to his foster mother, and he didn't even indulge in drinking or smoking habits.

Yet, Francis nurtured his admiration for the city's big-shot racketeers, such as Arnold Rothstein and Owney Madden. These were his real heroes, the guys whose names appeared almost daily in New York newspapers. They drove the best cars with surfaces polished to a sparkling shine, and their clothes were tailor-made and fashioned from only the most expensive material. But what Francis envied most was the respect these gangsters received from nearly everyone they met. When they walked into a nightclub or upper-class dining establishment, they were treated better than police captains or civic officials. Crowley noted that even up-and-comers, such as Dutch Schultz, Legs Diamond and Lucky Luciano, were given the same fawning attention by carhops and maitre d's. Francis understood that respect was directly proportionate to one's level of success, and that in the milieu of New York's underworld, those who received the best treatment were the guys who had made their "rep."

"Madden's a limey, and Rothstein and Schultz are Jews," Francis would tell himself. "If them foreigners can get peoples' respect, then I sure as hell can."

The major difference between Francis Crowley and the gangsters he hoped to emulate was that he was both impatient and reckless. He jumped into his criminal career with swift determination. He purchased a .38-caliber pistol as a birthday present for himself and teamed up with a simpleton he worked with named Rudolph Duringer, also known as "Big Rudolph" or simply "Fats."

Although Duringer had no real criminal ambition, Crowley easily convinced Fats to partner with him on a robbery spree. They worked their dreary day shift at the factory and then at night broke into small businesses in and around Manhattan. Their rewards were paltry, but Crowley was ecstatic to finally take the first steps towards fulfilling what he saw as his true destiny.

Crowley knocked over his first bank in early 1931, but it was a minor score, and he and Duringer continued with their bush-league holdups. Crowley was hoping that these burglaries might bring him to the attention of the same New York big shots who had given Schultz and Diamond opportunities. Such was not the case.

If Crowley was noticed at all by the city's underworld, he was regarded as an impulsive, trigger-happy punk of absolutely no value to the maturing criminal structure. Besides, they already had the psychopathic "Mad Dog" Coll* to contend with.

Crowley's frustration about his lack of status led to his first murder when he and Duringer robbed a grocery store and met with resistance from the owner. It galled Crowley not to be taken seriously by a mere grocery clerk, so he fired a single bullet at the man right between eyes.

Later, he shrugged, "What choice did I have?"

---

*Vincent "Mad Dog" Coll (1909–32) earned a reputation as the most violent killer of Prohibition New York. A former employee of beer baron Dutch Schultz, Coll tried to take over Schultz's empire and embarked on a bloody gang war, the violence reaching its climax in July 1932, when a gun battle claimed the life of five-year-old Michael Vengalli. Coll was later shot to death by Schultz gunmen.

Crowley wanted more than ever to have his reputation acknowledged by the city's chief racketeers—those who didn't have to resort to nickel-and-dime stickups and who always seemed to enjoy the best furnishings of life. Because he shared Jack "Legs" Diamond's Irish background, he began hanging around the same dancehalls that the flashy gangster was known to frequent, hoping for an introduction.

Crowley quickly grew impatient as Legs Diamond (probably hiding from his rivals) was a no-show. Then one night when his pal Duringer was rejected by a dancehall hostess named Virginia Banner for whom he had the hots, Crowley vented his anger and frustration by grabbing Virginia as she left work.

"So you're too stuck up for my pal, huh?" Crowley hissed.

The two gangsters shoved her into the rear seat of their car and drove off to a secluded spot where Duringer raped her repeatedly before Crowley ended the poor girl's misery by calmly blasting a bullet into her brain. Even though Virginia was dead, Duringer, caught up in the frenzy of the moment, demanded that Crowley then hand him the pistol, which he used to fire another shot into the girl's lifeless body.

The pair dumped her corpse, then drove back into the city. After Virginia's body was discovered, ballistics was able to match the bullets found in her with the slug fired into the grocery-store owner. The problem was that they lacked a suspect.

Crowley and Duringer carried on with their petty stick-ups. And then, on the night of May 6, 1931, two police officers drove towards a green coupe parked on a "lovers lane" spot known as Black Shirt Lane just outside North Merrick, New York.

Patrolman Frederick Hirsch smiled at his partner, Peter Yodice. "Probably just some kids. Better send 'em on home."

Hirsch grabbed his flashlight and walked towards the car. As he neared the driver's side, he shone the white beam through the window, settling on the faces of a teenage boy and his obviously startled girlfriend. Meanwhile, Yodice walked over to the front of the car to jot down the license plate number.

"You know you kids aren't supposed to be out here after dark."

The young man kept his brown eyes fixed on the officer.

"Would you show me your driver's license?" Hirsch requested.

The boy suddenly seemed confused. "License—? Oh, yeah, sure."

He removed his arm from around his girl's shoulder, and then in a swift movement, threw open the car door, slamming it into Officer Hirsch and knocking him to the ground. Before the patrolman could recover, Francis Crowley already had his .38 out and pumped three rounds into him. Crowley then leaped from the car to retrieve the dead officer's pistol, which he aimed towards Hirsch's partner. But Officer Yodice had already dashed for cover, and the cop fired off several shots as the green coupe slammed into gear and roared off into the darkness.

Yodice had recorded the license plate number and discovered that the coupe was registered to one Francis Crowley. In addition, the bullet the coroner dug out of Officer Hirsch matched the slugs found in both the grocery-store owner and Virginia Banner. The authorities had identified their murderer and issued a shoot-to-kill order.

The police went on an intense manhunt, but did not flush out Crowley. The teenage fugitive was ensconced in a cheap apartment on West 90th Street with Fats Duringer and Crowley's 16-year-old girlfriend, Helen Walsh, who had been with him the night of Hirsch's murder. There, Crowley devoured newspapers, delighting in the publicity surrounding his murderous exploits.

While the press fed Crowley's ego, reporters also worked diligently to uncover information that would assist in the capture of the elusive outlaw. A reporter with the *New York Journal* tracked down a friend of Crowley's named Billie Dunne, who had worked at one of Legs Diamond's dance-halls. When the reporter mentioned Crowley's name, the girl startled him with the vehemence of her reply.

"Don't you mention that bastard to me!" Billie screamed.

After she calmed down, the girl told the reporter that Crowley and his friends had forcibly "evicted" her from her own apartment.

"Can you give me the address?" the reporter asked.

Billie did not hesitate. "Sure, 303 W. 90th Street," she said.

The reporter barely had time to thank Billie before leaping from his seat to call the police with the information. Then he notified his paper, requesting that a news photographer join him at the site.

Before he left, the girl shouted a warning, "Watch yourself. That guy would shoot his own mother."

The photographer assigned to the story, Jerry Frankel, arrived before the reporter, and not having been properly briefed on his assignment, carried his camera equipment up five flights of stairs and casually knocked on the apartment door. A voice from inside told him to go him away, as if Frankel was a pesky salesman.

"Go on, get outta here. We don't want none."

Police detectives, who had already assumed positions in the hallway, hushed Frankel and hurried him away from the door before he could reply. Then two of the cops moved from their hiding places to get Frankel and his photography gear back towards the stairs.

Frankel soon learned how lucky he was. In the next instant, Crowley threw open the door to the apartment and let loose with a double dose of lethal gunfire. He was armed for combat; the two .38s he was brandishing were strapped to his hips while another pistol was secured in a shoulder holster. He had his trousers rolled up to the knees, revealing two more guns lashed to his legs.

The cops, who had urged Frankel down the stairway, dove for cover. Before they could draw their own weapons to return fire, Crowley had already exhausted his ammo supply and had slammed himself back inside the suite.

"Come and get me, coppers!" his high, reedy voice challenged them through the barricaded door.

The detectives knew that Crowley was desperate and that it would be suicide to charge the apartment, so they decided to wait for reinforcements.

Anticipating a shootout, converging police cordoned off two city blocks, while marksmen carrying machine guns, shotguns and rifles took up strategic positions along the street. Even with this formidable manpower, more police were summoned to the scene. A voice boomed through the bullhorn, ordering Crowley to surrender.

Crowley replied by opening fire.

The police unleashed their own artillery. Their relentless gunfire shattered the windows of Crowley's apartment and blasted away much of the building's wood and brick frontage.

Crowley responded like the Hollywood desperado he aspired to be. He jumped from window to window, a pistol in each hand, firing in a forward-and-backward rotation that would earn him his nickname, "Two Gun." He paused only long enough to reload his weapons, and then he was back at it, exchanging gunfire without letup. At one point, Crowley rushed out of the apartment to pour shots down both ends of the hallway, in case the cops were still planning to break down the door to get him. Meanwhile, a terrified Helen and Duringer took refuge under the bed.

"Yer both yella," Crowley said in disgust.

The ruckus drew hundreds of spectators to the scene. People were leaning out the windows of neighboring buildings to watch the action. Incredibly, many were cheering for the gunman. By now over 300 police officers were on the street trying to halt Crowley's rampage and at the same time control the 15,000 bystanders.

Crowley shouted curses out the window, challenging the cops to come inside and get him. Despite all his bravado, Crowley knew that there was no way out for him. When the shooting halted so that the police could prepare for a final assault, Crowley took advantage of the moment to scribble a farewell note. In it, he painted a pathetic picture of himself as an innocent drawn to a life of crime.

> *To Whom It May Concern:*
>
> *I was born on the 31. She* [Helen] *was born on the 13 (of October). I guess it was fate that made us mate. When I die put a lily in my hand, let the boys know how they'll look. Under my coat will lie a weary, kind heart that wouldn't hurt anything. I hadn't anything else to do, that's why I went around bumping off cops. It's the new sensation of the films. Take a tip from me to never let a copper go an inch above your knee. They will tell you they love you and as soon as you turn your back they will club you and say the hell with you. Now that my death is so near there is a couple of bulls at the door saying "come here." I'm behind the door with three .38—one belongs to my friend in North Merrick (Officer Frederick Hirsch)—he would have gotten me if his bullets were any good.*

Helen wrote her own letter in which she described the way she wanted to be presented in her casket if she should be killed. The police captain shouted a final warning to Crowley to give himself up.

Seconds later, Crowley spat out the window, "You ain't never gonna take me alive, ya dirty coppers!" He punctuated his promise with several blasts from his pistols.

At that, the captain gave the signal, and police fired into the apartment a volley of teargas shells, which exploded on impact and flooded the room with noxious fumes.

"Son of a bitch!" Crowley screamed, as he scrambled to retrieve the ruptured shells and toss them back out the window. He yelled for Duringer to help him, but the fat man remained cowering under the bed.

Outside, police sharpshooters were ready for Crowley to present himself as a target, and when the young killer appeared in the window the second or third time to toss out the ruptured teargas canisters, a fusillade of shots rang out, slamming into him. Crowley stumbled backwards and dropped to the floor. After several moments, he struggled to his feet, bracing himself against the wall and shooting wildly out the window.

With Crowley's attention focused completely on the street, a volunteer squad of police officers effected the second phase of the operation and stormed the apartment. Crowley twisted his body towards the door, but with his vision blurred by the tear gas, he aimed his pistols randomly, firing ineffectively and emptying both guns. Officers quickly overpowered him, and when he finally collapsed from the four bullet wounds he'd sustained, they hustled him from the apartment together with the trembling Duringer and Helen.

Miraculously, even though more than 700 bullets were expended during the shootout, Crowley was the only one who sustained injuries.

The Siege of W. 90th Street had ended, although the shootout was immortalized on the big screen the following year in Howard Hawks' brilliant *Scarface*, when gangster Tony Camonte tries to fight off the city's police force from inside

Francis "Two Gun" Crowley on his way to the hospital and ultimately to the Sing Sing death house following "The Siege of W. 90th Street"

his apartment building, only to be subdued by the law when overcome by tear gas.

Although Crowley was weak and barely conscious, police still strapped him securely to the stretcher before transporting him to a nearby hospital. Emergency surgery and blood transfusions saved his life but for little purpose. When he stood trial for murder, Crowley knew that his fate was sealed.

What did surprise him was how both Fats Duringer and especially his beloved Helen turned against him. While Helen's testimony got her released, the jury showed no sympathy for Duringer, who blamed all his criminal actions on Crowley, and indicted him for the first-degree murder of Virginia Banner.

Crowley sat through his trial both amused and flattered by all the attention. The courtroom was filled to capacity every day. He was thrilled with the desperado handle the press had pinned on him—Two Gun—and thereafter referred to himself by the name.

He laughed out loud when the inevitable death sentence was read. He laughed even harder when Fats Duringer was similarly condemned to death. All throughout the trial, Crowley enjoyed displaying his tough-guy image for the benefit of newspaper reporters, and they responded by writing how Two Gun Crowley would go to the chair with a sneer on his lips.

Crowley was sent to the death house at Sing Sing. From the moment he passed through the doors of the famed penitentiary accompanied by a dozen deputies, he donned his belligerent attitude. When jailers searched him, they found tucked into one of his socks a spoon handle that could have been shaped into a knife. Crowley's deputies were red-faced and at a loss to explain how he could have gotten a potential weapon past them.

Two Gun Crowley's reputation preceded him into Sing Sing, and the sad-eyed little criminal who had shot it out with more than 300 of New York's finest was regarded as a celebrity. Crowley's days were numbered, but he was not planning to go quietly. Determined to live up to the expectations of his fellow condemned, on his first night on the "row,"

The diminutive 105-pound Crowley plays up to his hard-edged image as he prepares to face indictment for the murder of patrolman Frederick Hirsch.

he treated them to a show by cursing out his guards before kicking over his food tray.

"Feed this slop to the warden," he growled.

A short time later, after receiving a disparaging letter from one-time girlfriend Helen Walsh, Crowley instantly went on a rampage not motivated by theatrics. He nearly destroyed his cell, somehow starting a fire, which guards rushed in to quell. Crowley took advantage of the moment and clubbed a guard unconscious in a brash attempt to escape. Other guards quickly overpowered him.

Warden Lewis Lawes, a compassionate man who hoped to provide some measure of comfort to his condemned prisoners, was forced to deal harshly with the incorrigible Crowley because his behavior was creating dissention among the other men. He ordered that Crowley's cell was to be stripped clean and all clothing to be removed from his person.

Crowley passed his days pacing his cell naked, his sole diversion coming from the shouts of encouragement he received from the other cellblock murderers. It seems ironic that it was only on death row that he finally got the respect and recognition denied him on the outside.

At lights out, the guards gave Crowley a mattress for the night, but removed it first thing in the morning. Crowley never complained about the warden's punishment; he vowed to maintain his defiant posture until the moment they pulled the switch.

Warden Lawes saw through Crowley's bravado. It had been his experience that such outward toughness was merely a façade based on a need for acceptance. Lawes ordered Crowley placed in isolation, where he was convinced the hard outer shell of Two Gun would start to crack, allowing glimpses into Francis Crowley's innermost self. The warden's plan was effective. Away from his applauding audience, the youngster began to mellow. Eventually, at Crowley's humbled request, Warden Lawes restored his clothing and bunk privileges.

Yet, Crowley's derring-do image refused to die, and when Crowley was taken to New York to testify in a review trial for old pal Rudolph Duringer, he instantly reverted to form, especially when his wisecracks prompted reactions from the gallery. He played his bravado to the hilt, as if acknowledging that this would be Two Gun Crowley's last public performance.

When Crowley returned to the penitentiary, Warden Lawes discovered that Crowley possessed artistic talents. While sitting out his final days, Crowley asked the warden for some light wood, from which he constructed amazingly detailed models of the George Washington Bridge and the Empire State Building, using only magazine photos as a guide. His last model was a rambling miniature replete with elevators and workmen that he called Crowley's Hotel.

As Crowley's execution date grew nearer, he began to confide in Warden Lawes, whom he had come to trust and regard almost as a friend. He spoke most often about his troubled life. He told Lawes how he looked on the police as his enemies and how he knew that when he purchased his first gun it would lead him to the electric chair.

"The thing is," Crowley confessed, "even if I got out tomorrow, I know I'd keep on killin' them stinkin' cops."

Despite Crowley's unrepentant attitude, Lawes felt sadness for the boy, whom he believed had somehow been failed by the system.

Crowley received numerous requests from newspapers for exclusive interviews, and one paper wrote a sensational biography offering Crowley the enormous sum of $10,000 if he would sign his name to the project to confirm its authenticity before publication.

"If my (foster) mom coulda had that kind of dough when I was a kid," Crowley ruminated to Warden Lawes, "things woulda turned out a whole lot different."

Francis Two Gun Crowley walked the green mile to the chair on January 21, 1931, just a few days before his 20th birthday. Upon hearing that 25 reporters were on hand to witness his execution, Crowley decided to give them their money's worth. His erstwhile partner Rudolph Duringer had been electrocuted just minutes before, and Crowley pondered the irony of their fates.

"Funny, ain't it?" he said to Warden Lawes. "All the time I'm shootin' it out with the cops, and he's hidin' under the bed. Then he hopes to save his fat ass by turnin' on me, and look who fries first?"

Crowley regarded the seat sourly and turned to the warden. "I got a favor to ask you."

"What is it?" replied the warden.

Crowley's expression twisted into the sneer the reporters at his trial had predicted he'd wear on this day. "Get me a rag so I can wipe off the chair after that rat sat in it."

Lawes knew that Crowley's request was merely a final display of the killer's bravado, and he ignored it.

Crowley's expression was cold as he looked out at those gathered and then seated himself in the chair. But before the attending guards could fasten the straps to his arms, Crowley halted the procedure to draw one last puff from the cigar he had been smoking. Then he contemptuously flicked it towards the witnesses, hitting one of the reporters on the forehead.

"Sons 'o bitches," Crowley muttered, loud enough to be heard.

Before the dreaded black hood was placed over his head, Warden Lawes asked Crowley if he had a last statement to make.

Crowley was silent for a moment, then his voice softened. "Give my love to Mother."

Seconds later, the switch was pulled, and the life, career and ultimately the legend of Two Gun Crowley sizzled into oblivion.

~◯C~

CHAPTER NINE

Roger "The Terrible" Touhy
(1898–1959)

"The bastards never forget."
–Dying words of Roger Touhy

ROGER TOUHY (pronounced Too-hee) wasn't really terrible, although he worked his own public relations campaign to create a threatening gangster image. His cold, dead-eyed appearance furthered that perception. His vulture-like profile, accentuated by a hooked nose and cruel mouth, gave him the look of a true predator. Reportedly, even the powerful Al Capone was intimidated by Touhy and treated him with more respect than he did his other enemies.

Touhy was almost a big shot during Prohibition. For a time he controlled the major bootlegging operation in the Chicago suburb of Des Plaines, but perhaps his major failing was that he was one of the few gangsters of the era who ran his business with a level of integrity, never resorting to deceit or treachery in his dealings.

Touhy may have looked rough, and he talked tough, but he was never the big shot he pretended to be, and following the repeal of Prohibition, he rapidly faded into obscurity. His attempts to insinuate himself into other profitable rackets

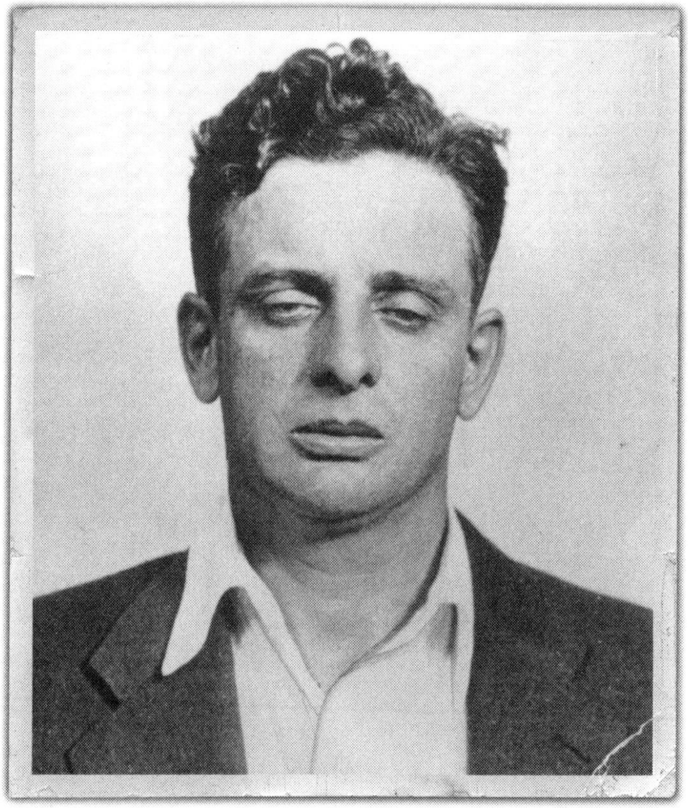

While not as tough as his reputation, Roger "Terrible" Touhy had a face that could inspire nightmares, as is evident in this, his first mug shot.

proved futile, and his audacious attitude with the Chicago underworld, then controlled by Frank "The Enforcer" Nitti, ultimately proved to be Touhy's downfall.

Nearly forgotten by the early 1940s, the spotlight refocused on Touhy while he was serving two consecutive life terms at Stateville Penitentiary in Joliet, Illinois. Twentieth Century-Fox studios chose Touhy's mediocre criminal career as the subject of their big-budget crime drama, *Roger Touhy, Gangster!* starring Preston Foster in the title role. Transplanted Chicago Syndicate gangster Johnny Roselli was listed as executive producer of the picture. ("Hollywood" Roselli would be murdered by the underworld in 1976, his body sawed in half and jammed into an oil drum that was later found floating in Florida waters.) The film received much ballyhoo and was even allowed a screening at the prison facility where Touhy was serving time.

Roger Touhy had become a celebrity, but at that point, Touhy neither wanted nor welcomed the fame. While safely ensconced in his jail cell, the ex-gangster knew there were still those on the outside who remembered him only too well.

It is debatable whether Roger Touhy would ever have become a criminal if not for a tragic accident that occurred when he was 10 years old. Roger Touhy (the original family spelling was "Tewy") was born in 1898, the youngest of eight children—two sisters and five brothers. He was raised in the Valley, a predominantly Irish community in Illinois. His father was a well-respected Chicago police officer, and by all accounts, Roger's lower-middle-class childhood was normal and uneventful.

All that changed when Roger's mother was killed when the kitchen stove exploded as she was preparing the family's dinner. Roger's father was a changed man following his wife's death. He moved his children to Downer's Corner, Illinois, and tried his best to build a new life. Although he tried to function as a single parent, raising eight children was difficult, and the youngsters were often left to fend for themselves.

Roger was also forever scarred by his mother's death. Yet, he was determined to please his father, and to that end, he became an altar boy at the local parish and worked odd jobs on weekends. His graduating class voted him class valedictorian at St. Joseph's Catholic School in 1911, whereupon he found a job as a telegrapher with Western Union. Roger was a good and conscientious worker, and he was soon promoted to manager of a small branch office.

He was content in his work, which was steady if lacking challenge. In 1915, Roger found a way to counter his boredom by becoming involved in union concerns, only to be fired by Western Union for his pro-labor activities. He worked for a brief time as an organizer for the Telegraph and Telecommunications Workers Union before once again settling into more routine employment as a telegraph operator with the Denver & Rio Grand Railroad in Colorado.

His experience in communications proved valuable when Roger enlisted in the navy at the onset of World War I. He was assigned to teach code to naval officers at Harvard, and after his discharge in 1918, he decided to go into business for himself. He managed to accumulate $25,000 as an oil-well speculator in Oklahoma, his capital earned primarily through purchasing and selling oil leases. He returned to his home state and opened a trucking company in Des Plaines, Illinois.

In 1922, Touhy married his childhood sweetheart, Clara, with whom he had two sons. He later lamented that he was never the husband and father he should have been because he was too ambitious and was always looking to hustle the next buck. Initially, Touhy ran his trucking business as a legitimate enterprise, but when Prohibition hit, he saw ways to further fatten his bankroll.

"I knew most of the bootleggers and saloon owners in my area," he wrote in his memoirs. "They were the guys who had the cash to buy fancy cars. If Chicago's best stores catered to them and their wives, why shouldn't Roger Touhy?"

Touhy began by hauling beer for local bootleggers, but it didn't take him long to realize that the real money was not in the delivery of alcohol, but in its manufacturing and distribution. Forming a partnership with a corrupt ward heeler named Matt Kolb, Touhy hired a chemist whom he instructed to brew the "best-tasting beer available in Chicago." Touhy ensured that only the finest ingredients went into his blend. At a time when many bootleggers were producing inferior-grade beer in order to turn a quick profit, Touhy would not compromise the quality of his product.

"We'll save money our own way," Touhy explained to Matt Kolb. "We'll keep makin' our beer the best so saloonkeepers will be coming to us to buy it, y'understand. We won't never need to hire no salesmen."

Touhy spared no expense in the manufacture and distribution of his "superior" beer. When profits started rolling in, he didn't become greedy. He reinvested the money in improvements to his company's brewing and distribution systems.

"We're unloading 1000 barrels a day," he boasted to his brother Eddie,* whom he had placed in charge of the brewery. "Figure it out, kid, we're bringing in $55 a barrel against our cost of $4.50."

Touhy was both clever and imaginative. When the Chicago police levied a 50 percent tax on the sale of his beer, he purchased a fleet of Esso gasoline delivery trucks. He kept the well-recognized logo on each vehicle and was able to make his beer shipments without police interference.

---

*By 1933, Roger and Eddie were the last surviving Touhy brothers. The other boys chose to remain in the Valley and had likewise taken up criminal pursuits under the gang leadership of "Terrible" Tommy O'Connor. Two were killed in mob conflicts, and another brother, Tommy, was crippled for life when he was felled by Syndicate machine-gun fire.

As his reputation grew, and the crooked authorities realized that they were no longer dealing with a penny-ante booze peddler, Touhy began brewing a "specialty" bottled beer exclusively for the local politicians and police as a "gift" to supplement the graft he was paying. Touhy even took an extra step by stamping personalized labels on the bottles. The gesture was much appreciated, and Touhy seldom had any trouble with the law afterwards.

While bootlegging was Touhy's most profitable enterprise, he also opened a bookmaking operation with Matt Kolb and his brother Tommy and later moved into the slot machine racket, distributing "one-armed bandits" to more than 200 outlets in Northern Cook County. It was a highly lucrative sideline, which, by 1926, was grossing more than $1 million a year.

Al Capone, at the height of his criminal power in Chicago, soon got wind of Touhy's bootlegging success and requested a meeting in Capone's plush headquarters at the Lexington Hotel.

"I hear you're pushin' a pretty good beer, but that you got a small market," Scarface Al said.

Touhy merely regarded Capone with a hard stare. "Why'd you send for me, Al?"

Capone spoke to the point. "My sources are, uh, temporarily dried up, an' I got some thirsty customers. I want delivery of 500 barrels to my various joints. But because I don't know how your product's gonna go over with my clientele, I want you should give me a discount rate."

Touhy knew Capone's market was vast, and he agreed to supply the 500 barrels at a reduced price of $37.50 apiece, knowing that he would still enjoy a substantial profit. Just a few days later, Capone called Touhy with an order of 300 more barrels. Touhy delivered them promptly.

The following Monday, Capone telephoned Touhy, who was to pick up payment the next day, as per their arrangement. Capone refused to pay him the agreed-upon price. His argument was that 50 of the barrels were "leakers."

"Forget it, Al," Touhy said, not about to lose $1900 on the deal. "I manufacture those barrels myself and haven't had a leaker yet." He went on to explain that each barrel was sealed with powerful air pressure to prevent such a problem.

"Don't try to chisel me," Touhy then warned.

Surprisingly, the gangster relented. "Okay, Rog. I'm just tellin' ya what I got told by the boys."

"I'll be by tomorrow to collect," Touhy said.

Touhy had played a dangerous gamble and won. Fortunately, Capone considered Touhy a more formidable threat than he actually was. Scarface had his boys do some checking, and their reports indicated that Roger Touhy not only had strong civic and police ties, but that he also had a squad of torpedoes at his disposal.

Of course, Touhy's reputation far outstripped the truth. He was just smart. For instance, Touhy's "generosity" to corrupt law officials was reciprocated on request with an impressive police arsenal that Touhy prominently displayed on his office wall whenever he was in negotiations with a difficult rival. Occasionally, during particularly heavy discussions, Touhy would arrange to have his toughest-looking truck drivers burst into the office to gather submachine guns to wipe out a fictitious enemy.

The tactic worked. Even such hardcore Capone gunmen as Murray "the Camel" Humphreys and Frank Nitti were so impressed by the drama that they advised Capone to walk softly with Roger Touhy.

But Capone wasn't listening. He was the absolute power in Chicago. He had already proven his eminence by his quick and efficient elimination of such potential usurpers as Dion

O'Banion, Hymie Weiss, Bugs Moran and even his two top double-crossing assassins John Scalise and Albert Anselmi. No, the mighty Al Capone would not allow a little-known upstart like Roger Touhy to challenge his underworld omnipotence.

"Capone envied me my anonymity, and he begrudged me my income," Touhy said in his 1959 biography.

Touhy maintained firm and total control over his own little fiefdom in Des Plaines by assisting the police in keeping out the lowlife criminal element. He proved himself to be a master of the "fix," be it with cash contributions or outright intimidation.

Capone once again saw his influence compromised when the crime czar focused his sights on Des Plaines, which he viewed as "virgin territory for whorehouses." This time Touhy's response was less a threat than friendly advice.

"This is a churchgoing community, Al. The guys in this town are all devout family men."

But the truth was that Touhy simply refused to give in to Capone. Later, when Scarface sent his chief henchman Frankie Rio and another gunman named Willie Heeney to meet with Touhy to further discuss his prospective brothels, Roger arranged for one of his burly drivers, who happened to be an ex-cop, to dress in appropriate gangster garb and, at a prearranged time, storm into the meeting, threatening to kill suspected Capone infiltrators.

Touhy shrugged, "Do what you think is best."

Touhy then kept up the performance by accepting a series of preplanned phone calls where he shouted decisive orders into the mouthpiece. By the time Touhy was through with his tirade, he was satisfied that he'd convinced Rio and Heeney of his sincerity in dealing with Big Al.

Al Capone dispatched other key men in his organization, such as "Machine Gun" Jack McGurn, to try to talk sense to

Touhy. In the lexicon of Capone's underworld, "talk sense" translated into: Either comply, or die.

But Touhy kept playing the percentages and coming out ahead. He continued with the charade, slipping his drivers a few extra bucks to parade through his office brandishing firearms whenever the Capone people were present.

Deciding against violence because he was under federal indictment for income tax evasion, Capone next tried to legally remove Touhy from the picture by fingering his rival in a police raid. The ploy failed, of course, because of Touhy's influence with local law enforcement.

Before Capone went to jail, he had his men kidnap Touhy's partner Marty Kolb, holding him for $50,000 ransom, which Scarface figured was a way to at least recoup his investment in Touhy's beer shipments.

Capone could play the game every bit as well as Touhy. His voice registered an equal measure of shock and sympathy when he personally made the call to Touhy, claiming that he was doing him a favor by acting as the go-between for the actual kidnappers. Touhy was not fooled.

Touhy was livid! He'd honored his agreement with Capone, providing him with a quality product and prompt service at a discount price, and then the scarfaced bastard had tried to cheat him! And Capone was sticking it to him again by shaking him down for a pocket-change ransom!

Roger Touhy might have had nothing more than his reputation to back him, but he realized that it was a formidable tool. After receiving the call from Big Al, he stormed into Capone's office alone.

Capone's first words to Touhy were: "I want you to know, Rog, I had nothin' to do with the snatch."

Touhy ignored the gang lord's transparent dissembling. He walked right up to Capone's desk and threw down an envelope containing the $50,000.

"Where's Matt?" he demanded.

Capone maintained his innocence, again insisting that he was merely acting as an intermediary. "I got nothin' against you or Matt, Rog. In fact, I'm tryin' to help you, ya know, takin' time outta my schedule to help straighten this out. Now, if you'll get outta here, Rog, I'll make the call."

Touhy smirked and left the office without a word. Capone's hoods soon released Kolb. Shortly thereafter, Capone went to jail, but the hostilities between the new leaders of the Chicago organization, specifically Frank Nitti and Murray Humphreys, and Roger Touhy escalated. In 1930, Touhy further infuriated the Mob by providing protection to the corrupt Irish labor unions that Capone was attempting to infiltrate. The dispute resulted in full-scale street warfare and the killing of about 100 men in a 12-month period. Matt Kolb was among the victims.

Touhy still had an ace in his hand because of his association with newly elected Chicago mayor Anton J. Cermak, who was every bit as corrupt as Capone's puppet mayor William Thompson. Although Cermak peppered his campaign speeches with promises to rid Chicago of rampant gangsterism, he was really working his own agenda, which included backing Touhy hoodlums against the Italian mob.

For a while, Touhy thrived under Cermak's crooked civic administration. But on December 19, 1932, the tide began to turn when two police detectives raided Frank Nitti's headquarters. They shot and seriously wounded the crime boss for resisting arrest. Later, testimony revealed that Anton Cermak had engineered the assassination attempt against Nitti to rid Chicago of the Capone mob's still-powerful control. He had forged a close association with Ted Newbury, a surviving member of the Bugs Moran crew who had taken control of the Irish mob following the St. Valentine's Day Massacre.

Unfortunately for Cermak, Frank Nitti survived and swiftly exacted his revenge. Newbury was murdered within weeks of the failed attempt. Then, on February 15, 1933, while appearing at a political rally for Franklin D. Roosevelt, Cermak himself was gunned down by a 31-year-old political radical named Joseph Zangara, who was then promptly tried and executed less than a month later.*

Touhy was scared. Without Cermak's political protection, he was an open target for mob retaliation. The new chiefs of the Chicago Outfit, Paul "The Waiter" Ricca and Anthony "Joe Batters" Accardo despised Roger Touhy for his open defiance of Capone and debated the best way to handle the upstart. It would have been a simple decision to have him killed, but Accardo was a man of vision. As he saw it, ordering the murder of Touhy might avenge an insult but would certainly preclude a later occasion when Touhy's reckless criminal exploits might prove beneficial to the organization.

The wisdom of this decision was realized in August 1933, when Touhy, Edward McFadden, Peter Stevens and Willie Sharkey were arrested by FBI agents and indicted for the kidnapping of brewing magnate William A. Hamm, Jr. The charge was totally false (as would later be verified by Alvin Karpis, one of the true perpetrators in the snatch). Indeed, it was a setup masterminded by the Chicago Mob to get Touhy and his gang out of the way.

---

*The target was commonly believed to be FDR, next to whom Cermak was sitting in an open car driving through the streets of Miami. Zangara reportedly shouted, "There are too many people starving to death!" before he opened fire. While Roosevelt was not injured, Cermak sustained two fatal bullet wounds. Zangara maintained to the end that FDR was his target and that he was acting alone, although it is speculated that he may have served as scapegoat in the Chicago Mob's revenge against Anton Cermak.

Because of all the negative publicity associated with Chicago during this period, the city's underworld was rarely eager to welcome gun-toting mavericks into its fold. Wildcat criminals who were afforded refuge in St. Paul and Kansas City were seldom embraced in Chicago.

The Barker-Karpis Gang was an exception. Despite their hillbilly beginnings, the band of renegade outlaws had managed through a profitable crime spree to amass sufficient funds that, with proper disbursement, guaranteed them protection, comfortable shelter, and when the need arose, even health care.

Another advantage the gang had over other desperadoes of the time was their willingness to take on strong-arm assignments. Freddie Barker, in particular, during these lay-low days was not averse to a little enforcement work, especially if the price and other inducements were right.

Roger Touhy's arrogance made him a most disposable commodity, valuable only as a fall guy to take the heat off the more profitable work the Chicago Mob now shared with the Barker-Karpis Gang. As a result, Touhy and several of his crew took the rap for a crime they did not commit. They were indicted by a grand jury on August 13, 1933, and went to trial, protesting their innocence against the FBI's assertion that they had a "strong, solid case" against the gang.

But the prosecution's arguments collapsed before the jury, and Touhy and two of his fellow accused were declared not guilty. The third crew member, Willie Sharkey, couldn't anticipate the jury's verdict and committed suicide in his cell at the Ramsey County Jail.

Touhy no sooner walked away from one kidnapping charge than he was smacked with another. This time the victim was a shady character named Jake "the Barber" Factor, who had significant ties to Capone (and was the half-brother of cosmetics giant Max Factor).

Acquitted of the William Hamm kidnapping, Touhy (far right), with accomplices Albert Kator, Edward McFadden and Gustaf Schafer, was framed by Frank Nitti for kidnapping Jake Factor.

Jake Factor, an international confidence man, was facing extradition to Great Britain for a series of stock swindles, when Frank Nitti came up with a scheme to help Factor stay extradition, while at the same time putting the hated Roger Touhy "on the spot."

The plan worked like a charm. Factor was "abducted" outside the Dell's Roadhouse in Morton Grove. He was taken to a safe house, where he was kept in comfort and plied with food and booze until the phony ransom was paid. Once released, Factor promptly fingered Touhy as his kidnapper. Because of the high-profile nature of the case, J. Edgar Hoover dispatched Melvin Purvis to locate the culprit, and Purvis soon apprehended Roger Touhy.

Purvis later said even before Factor named his abductor, "We assumed from the start, with no material evidence, that the Touhy Gang was responsible for the crime."

With Factor retained as a government witness against Touhy, lawyers stalled the proceedings just long enough for Factor to be held past the 60-day legal deadline by which a person not extradited within that period must be released.

Touhy was battling both federal charges and the machinations of the Chicago underworld, and this time his protestations of innocence went largely unheard. While his first trial resulted in a hung jury, a second jury convicted him (with perjured testimony), and Judge Michael J. Feinberg sentenced him to 99 years in the Illinois State Prison at Joliet.

With the troublesome Touhy out of the way, Frank Nitti, Murray Humphreys and the new rulers of the Chicago Syndicate quickly took control of the Des Plaines beer-running operation.

Touhy filed several motions to have his case reopened, but they were all denied without a hearing despite mounting evidence that supported his claim of innocence. Touhy was embittered by his frame-up, which stripped the gangster not only of his power, but also his wealth. In 1942, a despondent Touhy told his wife Clara to take their two sons and move to Florida.

Although Touhy was regarded as a model prisoner at Stateville, all was not well. He grew restless after eight years of incarceration. It ate away at the gangster's ego that his time behind bars had eroded his reputation and that he was now referred to by a number. So when lifer Eugene O'Connor (aka Jimmy O'Connor) approached him to participate in a prison break, Touhy agreed. He later wrote that he never expected the break to be a success, but that even its failure would provide him with another moment of glory.

O'Connor outlined the plan. As he explained it, the timing was perfect. With most of the country's focus on the war, no one would pay much attention to an old-fashioned jailbreak. But even more to their advantage was that most of the younger guards had been pressed into military service, so prisons like Stateville were forced to recall older men and even recruit pensioners to watch over the prisoners.

O'Connor, a perpetual prison escapee, had meticulously worked out all the details. For example, with food rationing being observed, many items that were limited to the public remained in abundance in the prison storehouses. O'Connor sweetened his bribe to the key tower guards by offering foodstuffs that Touhy, who worked kitchen duty, was able to obtain. These foodstuffs could later be sold for a handsome profit on the black market.

Arrangements were made through the brother of one of the cons in on the escape to have a trusty smuggle two pistols into the prison. These guns were hidden at the base of the prison flagpole and later carried inside the walls by the trusty, wrapped in the folds of the American flag, which was lowered each evening.

On October 9, 1942, Touhy, O'Connor, Basil "the Owl" Banghart, Edward Darlak, St. Clair McInerney, Martlick Nelson and Edward Stewart put their plan into action.

Touhy was performing his daily kitchen chores, awaiting the arrival of the prison laundry truck. Driver Jack Cito backed up to the bakery door to gather the bins of aprons, towels and baking smocks. Touhy, armed with scissors obtained from the tailor shop, leaped through the driver's door and threw Cito from the truck. He jumped on top of Cito, slashed at him repeatedly with the scissors and demanded the truck keys. When Cito finally found the breath to speak, he told Touhy that the keys were still in the ignition.

Touhy wasn't a violent man, and this was a rare act of aggression on his part, but he was committed to escaping from prison. He left the bleeding Cito twitching on the ground, got behind the wheel of the truck and drove to the machine shop where the others were waiting.

O'Connor tossed Touhy one of the smuggled .45s, and the two rushed into the workroom where they quickly disarmed guards Samuel Johnson and George Cotter. Basil Banghart, another hardcore lifer, ordered Johnson to unlock a set of ladders, which were then loaded onto the back of the truck with Cotter's assistance.

As the truck rumbled across the yard, its motor suddenly stalled. Touhy shouted at the 300-plus inmates who were crowded around watching the action to push the vehicle in order to jump-start the engine. They complied willingly, cheering when their efforts brought the old engine rumbling to life. With the truck once again mobile, the convicts and their two hostages drove towards the northwest corner tower. Guard Johnson refused to help the convicts assemble the ladders for their ascent to Tower 3, and they beat him unmercifully.

Touhy fired a single shot at the guardhouse, shattering the window and superficially injuring the guard with flying glass. The convicts grabbed two high-powered rifles and a pistol, along with 200 rounds of ammunition. Then, they calmly climbed down the tower stairs and made their getaway in a car waiting for them outside the wall.

They drove into Chicago, where Touhy's pals had secured the gang an apartment in a rundown tenement building on the city's west side. Ironically, the apartment was not far from the Valley neighborhood where Roger Touhy had spent his early childhood.

Despite O'Connor's prediction, however, the gang's escape was major headline news, for about a week, until the press began refocusing their coverage on overseas developments. Touhy figured they'd be okay, as long as they laid low and stayed focused. But after two months of confinement, some began to get edgy and restless. Nelson and McInerney were the most belligerent, complaining incessantly about their need for female companionship. Touhy tried to reason with the two, but Nelson wasn't listening. He finally threw a punch at McInerney, instigating a brawl that brought furious neighbors hammering on their door.

Although Touhy managed to placate the angry tenants and soothe the tensions between the two brawlers, he could see that he was sitting on a veritable powder keg. The following day, he went off on his own and found a small apartment where he reveled in time spent by himself. He contacted his brother Eddie, who had managed to stash $2500 in cash before Nitti took over the Touhy brewery.

"The heat's on you, Rog. I think you'd better beat it to Arizona," Eddie implored.

Touhy laughed. "You're looking at it the wrong way, kid. There's too much else goin' on right now for anyone to give a hang about me crashin' outta stir."

Eddie disagreed, and although his concerns were justified, he couldn't convince Roger. Newspapers might have back-paged their coverage of the Stateville prison break, but the eight escapees remained the focus of a nationwide dragnet, the most intense police manhunt of the war years.

Touhy used some of the $2500 to purchase a phony driver's license, social security card, and most importantly for the time, a draft card that classified "Robert Jackson" 4F, exempting him from military duty. Then Touhy bought a used car so that he could enjoy driving through the forest preserves of the Chicago area and going to the movies.

Then one day he received a visit from Owl Banghart, who was the only one of the escapees who knew where Touhy lived. Banghart invited Touhy to come back to the west side apartment for Thanksgiving dinner with the boys. Touhy agreed, and he soon moved back in. But it wasn't long before old dissentions arose among the gang members.

This time, the mercurial Martlick Nelson split from the others, returning to his home in Minneapolis, where his own mother turned him in to the FBI just hours after he arrived. A scared and angered Nelson didn't hesitate to inform on the gang. The news was relayed to Washington, where the FBI prepared to recapture the criminals.

J. Edgar Hoover arrived at the scene to supervise the raid personally. He was still chafing at Touhy's escape from prosecution in the William Hamm kidnapping. This, in Hoover's eyes, was another miscarriage of justice for which the FBI took the blame.

The Bureau's entry into the case required some delicate legal maneuvering. A prison break was not punishable under existing Illinois law unless serious injuries were incurred during commission of the break and/or crimes committed during an escapee's time at large. This law was changed in 1949.

To justify his office's involvement, Hoover took advantage of a federal law, requiring all men of military age to notify their draft board should their address change. Hoover conveniently ignored that Touhy was 44 and well past the draft age, and that his fellow escapees, as convicted felons, were not required to register for the draft.

Agents and sharpshooters took up positions around the building in anticipation of an all-out gunfight with the gangsters. Undercover agents from the Chicago office had already moved into suites in the building to monitor the criminals' activities.

At 11:20 PM on December 28, 1942, Eugene O'Connor and St. Clair McInerney were returning to their suite after an evening of grog sampling when six weapon-toting agents suddenly confronted them.

"Federal officers. Put your hands in the air!" came the command.

A drunken O'Connor pulled his pistol.

"We won't be taken alive, boy!" he shouted to McInerney in his heavy Irish brogue, and for him that was the case as he was quickly shot dead. St. Clair McInerney also resisted the agents' order to surrender and fell to their gunfire. The gunfire was so relentless that both men were blasted over the stairway banister and hit a total of 35 times.

Touhy and Owl Banghart arrived back at the apartment after the commotion was over and went straight to bed. At 5:00 AM the following morning, searchlights woke Touhy and Owl Banghart when they speared directly into the windows of the apartment. They barely had time to wipe the sleep from their eyes when they heard a voice amplified through a police bullhorn.

"Roger Touhy, federal officers. We have you surrounded. Unless you come out immediately, we will commence firing tear gas into the windows."

Banghart wanted to duke it out with the feds and take their chances, but Touhy said no. He told the Owl to call out a surrender. It was a somewhat inglorious arrest for Roger Touhy, clad as he was in fire red pajamas. Touhy and Banghart walked out the front door of the apartment building, backs to their captors with hands clasped behind their heads.

Surrounded by agents and a throng of newspaper reporters, J. Edgar Hoover moved boldly towards the men once they were safely handcuffed. Owl Banghart took a good long look at the chief G-man.

"You're Hoover," he finally said.

Hoover was flattered at the recognition, and he acknowledged with a nod.

"Ya know, it's funny," Banghart added, deadpan. "You're a lot fatter in person than you appear on radio."

The FBI returned the convicts to Stateville, where they were immediately placed in solitary confinement and fed a diet of bread and water. Although Touhy received no additional penalty for his own participation in the escape, the judge tacked an extra 100 years onto his original sentence by invoking an Illinois law stating that any person assisting a state convict in a prison escape will likewise assume that prisoner's sentence.

Touhy feared dying a nobody, but quite the opposite occurred after his return to prison. First, came the popular film biography, and then in the 1950s, his lawyers received the support of many influential people who believed Roger was innocent of the Jake Factor kidnapping. Under such pressure, Federal Judge John P. Barnes reviewed the case and concluded that Factor had not been kidnapped at all and that the whole incident had been a masterfully designed hoax.

The media and civic groups criticized Judge Barnes for his decision, yet he further stated that the motivation for the bogus kidnapping was Factor's desire to stay extradition proceedings. He called into question Factor's character by stating that the alleged victim had recently served a five-year term in a federal penitentiary in Minnesota for attempting to swindle priests and others out of $1 million. Despite Judge Barnes' persistent efforts, it wasn't until 1959, after serving 17 years in prison, that Roger Touhy was finally granted release from Stateville.

Capone was dead, as was Frank Nitti. But Touhy knew that, in the Syndicate, old grudges never die. This was proven on December 17, 1959, just 23 days after his release from Stateville. As Touhy was entering the front door of his sister's house, several well-directed shotgun blasts blew apart most of his lower body. An ambulance came quickly, but as Touhy lay on the porch bleeding profusely, he accepted the inevitable.

"I've been expecting it," he said. "The bastards never forget."

Roger Touhy died in hospital four hours later.

As in so many gangland rubouts, the question remains: Who was behind the killing? Frank Nitti had committed suicide many years earlier, and the reigning boss of the city's underworld, Tony Accardo, had no personal grudge against

A visibly relieved Roger Touhy prepares for release after serving more than 20 years in prison.

Touhy. But a mob hit could not be sanctioned in Chicago without Accardo's approval.

Roger Touhy's murder was most probably ordered by long-time nemesis Murray "the Camel" Humphreys and might have been motivated by financial considerations. Humphreys had entered into a lucrative stock partnership with Jake Factor, who was trying to establish himself in Las Vegas and wanted to eradicate the Touhy connection from his past.

Another theory is that Touhy signed his own death warrant because he decided to file a $300 million suit against the State of Illinois for wrongful imprisonment. Such a lawsuit would have necessitated testimony from the city's top-ranking underworld names, none of whom were willing to speak on Touhy's behalf.

As an associate of Touhy's later remarked, "If Roger had just let sleeping dogs lie and maybe moved away to Florida, none of this would have had to happen."

The key figure in the fall of Roger "the Terrible" Touhy fared much better. Jake Factor made a fortune in real estate. He contributed substantially to John F. Kennedy's 1960 presidential campaign, and his generosity was rewarded with a full presidential pardon in 1962. He remained an active political supporter, backing both Hubert Humphrey and Richard Nixon until his death in 1984.

CHAPTER TEN

George "Machine Gun" Kelly
(1895–1954)

"No copper will ever take me alive."
–Machine Gun Kelly

RARELY HAS AN OUTLAW BEEN LESS DESERVING of his reputation than George "Machine Gun" Kelly. Yet no gangster ever embraced his image more. His tough-guy persona was as much a fabrication as his nickname. His brief criminal career was motivated mainly by professional vanity and manipulated by others' opportunism.

During the 1930s, newspapers had a field day exaggerating his outlaw exploits. The sensationalized headlines were mostly the invention of reporters and editors who recognized the commercial value in exploiting a criminal tagged "Machine Gun." The FBI also got into the act as Kelly's notoriety grew, branding him a "public menace" and another of J. Edgar Hoover's "rats to be exterminated."

In truth, George Kelly was an amiable if rather thickheaded lowlife whose criminal adventures were mostly as uninspired as his personal character. While he may have been the most physically imposing of the Depression Day Desperadoes, standing 6'1" and heavyset, he was certainly the least

Despite his moniker, "Machine Gun," George Kelly was really a happy-go-lucky Irishman whose only ambitions were to drink and try to live up to his wife's expectations.

intimidating. Kelly, although a braggart, was basically a harmless soul who didn't even like guns.

And because he lacked the brains of a Dillinger or a Karpis, his career was short, and he actually holds the distinction of being the first of the era's big-name criminals to be brought to justice. Unlike the blaze-of-glory demises of Baby Face Nelson, Pretty Boy Floyd and Bonnie and Clyde, Kelly's apprehension was anticlimactic. Despite all his bravado and tough talk about "never being taken alive," Machine Gun Kelly gave himself up without even reaching for his trademark tommy gun.

The system hastened to put him away, probably to set an example for other public enemies that justice would be swift and harsh. His arrest, extradition, trial and conviction remain one of the fastest on record, all occurring within the span of 18 days. Surrendering himself was the only smart move Kelly ever made. It allowed him to survive the era.

He probably wouldn't even rate footnote status among the decade's other more colorful lawbreakers were it not for his wife Kathryn. She was the true author of the Machine Gun Kelly legend. Kathryn was a shrewd woman whose obsession for power and a lavish lifestyle was far beyond the meager ambitions of her tough-talking but incompetent husband. It was she who prompted Kelly into his sole criminal triumph.

Machine Gun Kelly differed from his gangster contemporaries right from the start because he was raised in urban privilege, not rural poverty. Born George Kelly Barnes on July 18, 1895, in Chicago, Illinois, the son of a well-to-do insurance executive, young George was not lacking in financial comforts, although his was not a particularly happy childhood.

Two years after George's birth, the family moved to Memphis, Tennessee. His father was often absent, which George attributed to long hours at work. But teenage George discovered a disturbing truth when he caught his father entering the home of a woman with whom he'd been having an affair.

George adored his mother and decided not to tell her about what he had seen. Instead, he thought of how he might profit from his father's indiscretion. The following day, George skipped school and brazenly walked into his father's insurance office demanding an increase in his allowance and car privileges in exchange for his silence. His father, shocked as much by George's audacity as he was by his blackmail, had little choice but to go along.

George was impressed by his newfound power of persuasion. He thought that if he could employ it so effectively against his old man, then he could also use it to open other venues for himself.

While in high school, George took further advantage of his carte blanche automobile usage by dabbling in the bootleg trade. (Tennessee's state prohibition began in 1909). In his sophomore year, George was arrested for possession of alcohol. He called his father to bail him out, which he promptly did, using his considerable influence. Beyond such incidents, however, George had little contact with his father. Their relationship remained strained, and following the death of his mother, Elizabeth Kelly Barnes, shortly before George finished high school, their estrangement became permanent.

Although certainly no scholar, George honored his mother's wishes by enrolling at Mississippi State University where he intended to study agriculture. But George was bored with school, and his lack of interest showed in his grades. He dropped out of college after only four months.

He returned home to Memphis, where he capitalized on his father's reputation to ingratiate himself among the social elite. At one society gathering, he met a young woman named Geneva Ramsey, whose father was a prominent businessman. George and Geneva began seeing one another, much to her father's dismay. But after the two eloped, Ramsey reluctantly offered his new son-in-law a job with his construction company. Working side by side, the two men gradually developed a mutual respect, with Ramsey becoming almost a father figure to George.

However, after Ramsey was killed in a freak accident in the mid-1920s, a devastated George began to drink heavily, and his drinking took a toll on his marriage. His mother-in-law tried to help by selling her husband's company and loaning George money so that he might go into business for himself. But George's two entrepreneurial endeavors failed miserably, as did his other attempts at legitimate employment. It was as if all of his limited ambition had drained out of him with Ramsey's death. In his frustration, the easygoing George became physically abusive not only to Geneva, but to his first-born son, George, Jr., whom they nicknamed Sonny. (In later years, Sonny recalled his father's violent episodes and cut his dad out of his life entirely, much as George had done with his own father.)

With few options left open to him, George returned to bootlegging, which by the mid-1920s had become a highly lucrative business in Tennessee. Unfortunately, George was a better customer than salesman, and before long, he grew careless and was arrested for violating the state prohibition law. A furious Geneva was forced to borrow $200 from her mother to bail him out.

Geneva separated from George on many occasions, but always went back to him when he turned on his naïve charm and promised to straighten out his life. During one such estrangement, George rode out to Kansas City where he secured menial but honest work as a checker in a grocery store. He sent for his wife and children (a second son, Bruce, had since been born to the couple), but before long Geneva discovered that George was stealing from the store. This time she left him for good, returning to Memphis where she filed for divorce.

A drunken and despondent George attempted suicide by ingesting bichloride of mercury. In his delirium, he then called his father to ask if he would handle the funeral arrangements, to which the old man replied, "Gladly, son."

Later, as George recovered in the hospital, his father materialized at his bedside. Rather than offering sympathy and support, he used the occasion to turn the tables on his erstwhile blackmailing son, berating him for his failed effort and advising him to use a gun next time.

George remained in Kansas City, where he set up a small bootlegging business. Dropping his father's surname, he thereafter referred to himself as George R. Kelly. He and his partners enjoyed fast success in their alcohol-running enterprise, due in no small part to the people they employed— men of honest character whom they paid well to insure their loyalty. They were soon able to expand their operations into Texas, Oklahoma, Tennessee, Mississippi and eventually into New Mexico.

Kelly enjoyed his work, which gave him good profit for little work and little risk. Although he rarely ran into resistance from his small-town customers, who were mainly druggists, he adopted a tough-talking demeanor, which he'd picked up from real gangsters he had met. Kelly's gravelly, side-of-the-mouth delivery coupled with his bouncer-like physique always signaled the use of strong-arm persuasion.

But Kelly's major failing was that he'd never possessed an edge to his personality, which most criminals employed to their advantage both in the commission of crimes and in staying ahead of the law. When things ran smoothly, Kelly would relax, get drunk and let his guard down. And that was exactly what happened when he was arrested in Santa Fe on March 14, 1927, and sentenced to three months in the New Mexico State Prison for bootlegging.

On his release, Kelly saw that his minor bootlegging empire had dissolved along with his partners. He moved to Tulsa, Oklahoma, where he was picked up for vagrancy on July 24, 1927. Desperate to make a few bucks, Kelly committed his most serious crime. He was arrested for selling liquor on an Indian reservation, a federal offense that landed Kelly three years in Leavenworth Federal Penitentiary.

While in prison, Kelly became acquainted with many big-league bank robbers, including Charlie Harmon, Francis "Jimmy" Keating, Thomas Holden and Frank "Jelly" Nash. But Keating and Holden weren't around long enough to teach the eager Kelly the tricks of their trade. Using forged trusty passes, the two convicts walked out of the prison in late February 1930. Because Kelly had been chummy with the pair, and his work duty had him assigned to the photography department of Leavenworth's record section, authorities at first suspected him of complicity in the escape. Kelly, of course, denied the accusation, and because there was no strong evidence against him, no charges were laid.

Kelly was released from Leavenworth later that same year, and he immediately headed to St. Paul, Minnesota. Accompanying him was the woman who changed his life forever.

Born Cleo Brooks in Saltilo, Mississippi, in 1904, she was a pretty, dark-haired girl who knew from childhood exactly what she wanted, and that was a life far removed from the poverty in which she was raised. She'd obviously inherited her questionable character from her mother, who one day simply deserted her husband to take up with a man of slightly better means, a rancher named R.G. "Boss" Shannon.

At 15, Cleo married a laborer with whom she had a daughter, Pauline. Two divorces later, the renamed "Kathryn" met small-time bootlegger Charlie Thorne. Their marriage was both passionate and volatile. The union ended in 1927 when Charlie hurriedly scribbled a note that read, "I can't live with her or without her, hence I am departing this life," and he fired a bullet into his temple.

Even though the word "hence" didn't exist in Charlie's vocabulary, and a gas station attendant later testified that an irate Kathryn had threatened to kill her husband after she'd discovered him cheating, the coroner's jury ruled Charlie Thorne's death a suicide.

Acquaintances described Kathryn as a tough customer, and she was arrested on several occasions, spending time in jail for shoplifting and prostitution. She frequented speakeasies and was known to out-drink her male companions.

Kelly met Kathryn in 1927 through their mutual acquaintance "Little" Steve Anderson, an Oklahoma bootlegger. Kelly worked for Anderson, and Kathryn was Anderson's mistress. There was a strange but instant attraction between the rough-edged Kelly and the coldly calculating Kathryn, but their romance was put on hold while George sat out his three-year stretch in Leavenworth. Upon his release in 1930, George married Kathryn, and she immediately went to work fashioning a profitable image for her new husband.

The story goes that it was Kathryn who bought George his first Thompson submachine gun and insisted on daily practice at her stepfather's 500-acre ranch in Paradise, Texas, until he became a marksman. She also started the rumor that George actually had learned his proficiency with a machine gun during combat in World War I, even though George faked a medical deferment in college to avoid the draft.

Following each of Kelly's target practices, in which he reputedly learned to shoot walnuts off a fence at 25 yards without scraping the paint, Kathryn collected the spent cartridges and handed them out to friends as souvenirs.

"These were fired by Machine Gun Kelly," she would say in a conspiratorial whisper. "Remember that name—Machine Gun Kelly."

Kathryn was so convincing in promoting her husband's hardboiled image that even many of her underworld acquaintances remained wary and respectful of Machine Gun Kelly.

Although Kelly savored and flaunted his new reputation, booze was still more important to him. Kathryn explained her

husband's frequent absences by saying that he was off somewhere pulling a big job, when in truth, Kelly was usually in
the back room of the ranch house either sleeping off a hangover or battling a case of delirium tremens.

On July 15, Jimmy Keating and Thomas Holden sought out
Kelly to repay him for helping them escape from Leavenworth.
They invited him to join them in knocking over the Bank of
Willmar, Minnesota. Rounding out the team would be bank-
robbing heavyweights Harvey Bailey, Verne Miller and Sammy
Silverman. Kelly was both proud and pleased to be included in
such company, and he was determined to do his part—at
Kathryn's urging, of course.

The heist was a great success. The outlaws escaped with an
estimated $70,000. But the robbery was reportedly also one of
the most vicious bank attacks in Minnesota history. One of
the gang brutally pistol-whipped a cashier during the heist,
and while making their escape, another fired his machine gun
into a group of onlookers, wounding two women and killing
a security guard. While it is doubtful that Kelly fired the random shots, Kathryn beamed with pride whenever she over-
heard someone say that it was Machine Gun Kelly who was
responsible for the shooting.

Violence also erupted within the gang following the
holdup. On August 14, 1930, Sammy Silverman and two associates were found murdered in a lover's lane area near Wild-
wood Park in Minnesota. Their assassin was presumably Verne
Miller, who later claimed to Kelly that Silverman had double-
crossed him. It is more likely that ex-cop Miller wanted a bigger
piece of the take.

Kelly's next job was in September when he participated
in a bank robbery in Ottumwa, Iowa. The following year
Kelly and Kathryn moved to Fort Worth, where they stayed
at the home of Kathryn's deceased ex-husband, Charlie
Thorne. On April 8, 1931, Kelly along with Keating, Holden and

powerhouse recruits Freddie Barker, Frank Nash and Lawrence DeVol robbed the Central State Bank of Sherman, Texas, for a mere $40,000.

Kelly then partnered with ex-convict Albert L. Bates to knock over the First Trust and Savings Bank of Colfax, Washington, for a take reported to be $77,000—his biggest payday ever. By this time, the police were on to the outlaw, and they raided the Kellys' Fort Worth home, only to find that the couple had already fled.

Kelly's last known bank robbery occurred on November 30, 1932, when he and Al Bates robbed the Citizen's State Bank of Tupelo, Mississippi, for a mere $38,000. Kelly's growing lack of interest in bank heists and Kathryn's frustration over their paltry profits due to the country's Depression prompted the Kellys to seek a new criminal direction.

But Kelly was lazy. He much preferred drinking to working, yet he was constantly reminded that he would have to bring in money if he wanted to keep Kathryn happy. In contrast to her husband's lethargic nature, Kathryn was a dynamo. It is commonly accepted that she not only assisted in the planning of many of Kelly's bank robberies, but that she even participated, disguising herself as a man and acting as an armed getaway driver.

One morning, while Kelly was nursing his usual hangover, Kathryn proposed a kidnapping scheme.

"Kidnappin'?" Kelly replied in his whiskey-thickened growl as he poured himself a shot of the "hair of the dog."

Kathryn quickly showed him the various press clippings she had been amassing, each of which showed the profitability in such a venture. The recent William Hamm kidnapping, for example, had netted the culprits $100,000.

At first, Kelly was doubtful. The year before, on July 22, he and partner Eddie Doll abducted South Bend, Indiana banker Howard Woolverton. They had released him after two days of aimless driving when Woolverton told the kidnappers that he didn't have the money to pay the ransom, but that he would certainly raise the funds if he was released. Of course, Kelly's follow-up demands for payment went unanswered.

Even after that fiasco, Kathryn still felt her husband could pull off a successful kidnapping. She eventually convinced him with the same persuasion she had employed to make others believe Machine Gun Kelly was the most dangerous criminal in America.

Next, they had to decide on a target. Kathryn had initially considered abducting a prosperous Indiana businessman, but she sabotaged her own plan when she got drunk one night and shot her mouth off to two men she'd invited to a party at the Shannon ranch. The men turned out to be Fort Worth detectives Ed Weatherford and J.W. Swinney, and police quickly blanketed the businessman with security.

Ironically, the situation turned out well for the would-be kidnappers because it was later discovered that the "wealthy" businessman had gone broke and would never have been able to raise a substantial ransom. But it didn't take Kathryn long to select a better prospect—Charles F. Urschel, millionaire oilman from Oklahoma City. And while Kelly sat in a back room drinking himself into oblivion, Kathryn carefully laid the groundwork for the snatch.

Shortly after 11:00 PM on the night of July 22, Kelly and Al Bates burst onto the front porch of the Urschel home where Urschel and his wife were playing cards with neighbors. Bates brandished a pistol, and Kelly pointed his tommy gun at the group.

Urschel, a man who had achieved his success through grit and hard work, was not easily intimidated. He stood up to face the intruders and began to speak.

Kelly aimed his machine gun at him and snarled, "Don't be a hero." He then asked, "Which one of you's Urschel?" Spoken in Kelly's exaggerated gangster vernacular, he certainly must have pronounced the name "Oischel," like his favorite Hollywood hoodlum of the time, Barton MacLane.

One of the women screamed, and Kelly swung his machine gun towards her.

"Shaddup! Scream one more time, an' I'll blow your heads off," he threatened.

Kelly again asked Urschel to identify himself. But neither Urschel nor the only other male in the group, neighbor Walter Jarrett, acknowledged him.

"All right, then we'll take the both of yuh," Kelly said, as he gestured the two men away from the house with the barrel of his machine gun.

Both Urschel and Jarrett remained calm, assuring their wives that they would be all right.

"Well, we'll just see 'bout dat," Kelly smirked.

He ushered the men into the backseat of the car, keeping his machine gun trained on them. Bates got behind the wheel of the still-idling car, and they drove off into the clear Oklahoma night. Kelly waited until they'd driven several miles out of town before checking the men's wallets for identification. He withdrew the $51 Jarrett had in his billfold, then ordered Bates to pull off on the shoulder of the road where they let Jarrett out.

"Look at it dis way," Kelly side-smiled at Jarrett before slamming the car door on him. "Da way youse was playin' cards, yuh woulda lost it anyway."

The afternoon following the kidnapping, Kelly, Bates and their blindfolded captive arrived at their hideout—the Shannon ranch. Later they took Urschel to a small shack where Shannon's son Armon lived with his wife. There, they handcuffed him to the leg of a baby's highchair and forced him to sleep on a quilt on the floor.

What the Kellys didn't realize was that Urschel was not only powerful in wealth but also in political influence. He was a friend of newly elected president Franklin Delano Roosevelt who, on receiving word of Urschel's abduction, demanded immediate results from J. Edgar Hoover and the FBI.

Federal legislation had been passed following the Lindbergh kidnapping expanding the FBI's jurisdiction and allowing agents to go after kidnappers. Hoover dispatched key men on the trail of Urschel's abductors just hours after receiving a frantic call from Urschel's wife. As with nearly every crime committed in the Oklahoma territory during the early 1930s, the Bureau's first suspect was Pretty Boy Floyd (who had already been blamed for some of Kelly's bank jobs).

They soon eliminated Pretty Boy Floyd from their list because he had disappeared from Oklahoma in the aftermath of the Kansas City Massacre just one month earlier. The agents quickly had the Bureau check out their files for other possible candidates. Machine Gun Kelly did not even make their short list.

All that would soon change. Presumably it was Kathryn who arranged the details for delivery of the ransom money. The payment was to be made in "genuine used federal reserve currency." Urschel's friend, E.E. Kirkpatrick, would act as the go-between. The kidnappers told him that on the evening of July 29, he was to board the Sooner train, which traveled from Oklahoma City to Kansas City. They instructed him to stay alert for two field fires on the right side of the tracks. At the second bonfire he was to toss the briefcase containing the ransom money from the observation car. The ransom note guaranteed that Urschel would be nearby and released once the kidnappers had the money in hand.

The clever plan backfired when Kelly (who, contrary to the gang's promise, did not have Urschel) flooded the engine of the car in his eagerness to get to the site and arrived too late to set the field fires. He stood by dumbfounded as the train and the ransom money sped past him.

Kathryn, perhaps anticipating that her husband would somehow botch the pickup, had prepared an alternate plan. If the train drop went awry, Kirkpatrick was to go on to Kansas City and register at the Muehlebach Hotel to await further instructions. On Sunday at 5:45 PM, he received a telegram instructing him to take a cab to the La Salle Hotel and walk west down Lincoln Avenue holding the cash-filled briefcase in plain sight in his right hand. As he walked, Kirkpatrick was suddenly accosted by a nervous-looking, dark-complexioned, heavyset man wearing a stylish summer suit, two-tone shoes and a brim-lowered Panama hat.

"I'll take dat bag, Mr. Kincaid," Kelly said, referring to Kirkpatrick by his cover name.

Kirkpatrick was cautious. "How do I know you're the right man?"

"You know goddamn well I am," Kelly growled.

"Two hundred thousand dollars is a lot of money," Kirkpatrick said, maintaining a rational tone. "I must know that Mr. Urschel will not be harmed."

Kelly was growing impatient. "Just hand over da money. My boys is waitin' in da car." (His "boys" was accomplice Albert Bates).

Kirkpatrick was insistent. "Just as soon as I have a definite answer to give Mrs. Urschel. When will her husband be released?"

"He'll be home in 12 hours," Kelly told him. Kelly didn't know that Kirkpatrick's stall was not just a way to ascertain and hopefully assure Urschel's safety, but was intended for later identification purposes. Kelly, typically, had given no thought to disguising his appearance, and Kirkpatrick noted a great deal during their brief conversation.

Kirkpatrick then dropped the bag to the sidewalk and walked away without turning back.

Kelly retrieved the bag and hurried to the car where Al Bates was waiting.

"Let's scram outta here," the perspiring Kelly said.

They sped back to the Shannon ranch. Kathryn was pacing the floor and rubbing her palms in anticipation. She'd already made extensive plans on how she would spend both her and George's share of the ransom money. She had also decided to kill Urschel.

"We ain't killin' no one," Kelly responded to his wife's suggestion, pointing towards the stacks of bills on the kitchen table. "We got da money, an' I gave Kincaid my word."

Kathryn, impressed at her husband's uncharacteristic assertiveness, was persuaded to release Urschel.

Meanwhile, Urschel had not been sitting idly. Although blindfolded, he carefully compiled a list of mental checkpoints for later reference. He noted that twice each day he could hear airplanes flying overhead. He would then wait five minutes before casually asking his captor what time it was, thereby determining the daily 9:45 AM and 5:45 PM flight times, which were valuable in helping to narrow his location.

He also detected a distinct mineral taste to his drinking water and the sound of a pump from which the water was obviously drawn. In addition, he made a point of pressing his fingerprint on all reachable surfaces. More importantly, he initiated conversations with Kelly, and the thick-headed hood often revealed valuable bits of information.

"Dis place is as safe as it can be. After any of da boys pull a bank job, dey all come here to use it."

On July 31, nine days after his abduction, Urschel was released just outside Oklahoma City. During the drive, Kelly uttered threats against him doing any talking. He then handed Urschel a $10 bill and told him to walk to a nearby filling station and call a taxi to take him home.

Kelly and Kathryn, together with Al Bates, left Texas for Minneapolis, where Bates parted company with the pair. The Kellys sold a portion of their ransom loot, but because the money was hot, it would take a while to find a fence willing to handle the rest. Broke and impatient, the Kellys decided to take their chances. They embarked on a wild spending spree, throwing money around without care or concern. Giddy with their success, they seemed unaware that with each dollar spent, they were playing a dangerous game of Russian roulette.

The couple often found themselves shutting down saloons or speakeasies. Although Kathryn had a high tolerance for alcohol, she could never keep up with her husband. Often a vaguely sober Kelly would have to slap his wife silent when, fueled with equal portions of gin and pride, she would start to brag about their recent kidnapping endeavor.

Unbeknownst to Kathryn, the Urschel kidnapping had also sparked a renewed interest from the two Fort Worth detectives, Weatherford and Swinney, whom she had earlier tried to coax into her employ. Thinking that there might be a connection between the Urschel snatch and her drunken proposition made that night at the Shannon ranch, the detectives dutifully notified the FBI, who immediately mobilized their resources and flew into Texas. (Alvin Karpis later said that two local police officers, neither of whom he named, were actually participants in the kidnapping, but that they turned on their partners when they were cut out of their share of the ransom.)

Charles Urschel offered his full co-operation in tracking down his abductors. His resourcefulness while in captivity led agents directly to the Shannon ranch and the little shack where he was held. Realizing that the jig was up, Armon Shannon confessed his complicity in the crime and named both his sister and her husband as the true masterminds behind the kidnapping.

The agents hit further pay dirt when they arrested bank robber Harvey Bailey, who was recuperating at one of the dilapidated cottages on the property after being wounded in the leg during a gunfight. Agents discovered that he had $1200, $500 of which was identified as marked ransom money.

On August 12, the same day the Shannon ranch was raided, Albert Bates was arrested at a hotel in Denver for selling money orders taken during the Tupelo bank heist the previous year.

By mid-August, just two weeks after the release of Charles Urschel, the government was preparing its case against the co-conspirators in the kidnapping, which included "Boss" and Ora Shannon, Armon and his wife Oletha, Al Bates and five money purchasers from St. Paul. Harvey Bailey was also charged as an accomplice, even though it is more likely that the marked money he'd had in his possession was a debt repaid by Kelly.

On August 18, Kathryn sent the following note to the Oklahoma Assistant Attorney General:

> *The entire Urschel family and friends and all of you will be exterminated soon. There's no way I can prevent it. I will gladly put George Kelly on the spot for you if you will save my mother who was innocent of any wrongdoing. If you do not comply with this request there is no way in which I can prevent the most awful tragedy.*
>
> *If you refuse my offer, I shall commit some minor offense to be placed in jail so that you will know that I have no connection with the terrible slaughter that will take place in Oklahoma in the next few days.*

Kelly naturally had no knowledge of his wife's attempted betrayal. But he, too, was so incensed at the arrest of his in-laws that he began writing threatening letters directed to Charles Urschel, whom he believed he had treated fairly, and indeed, whose life he had saved.

Ignorant Charles:

If the Shannons are convicted look out, and God help you for He is the only one that will be able to do you any good. In the event of my arrest I've already formed an outfit to take care of and destroy you and yours the same way as if I was there. I am spending your money to have you and your family killed—nice, eh? You are bucking people who have cash— planes, bombs and unlimited connections both here and abroad…Now, sap, it is up to you. If the Shannons are convicted, you can get you another rich wife in Hell because that will be the only place you can use one. Adios, smart one.

Your worst enemy,

George R. Kelly

I will put my prints below so you can't say some crank wrote this.

It has been surmised that Machine Gun Kelly wanted to be arrested and that his fingerprint postscript was a way of leading the authorities to him. He was tired of his life on the run. What's more, he was tiring of his relationship with the demanding Kathryn.

The couple raced across state lines to stay ahead of the law. While neither George nor Kathryn would subject themselves to plastic surgery, both bleached their hair blond. Using Chicago as their main center, the two continued to indulge in a plush lifestyle, until their carefree spending brought them to the attention of vigilant federal authorities. Forced to take it on the lam, Kelly and Kathryn returned to Memphis, where they were put up by a longtime pal named Jack Tichenor.

The criminal career of Machine Gun Kelly ended on the morning of September 26, 1933, when Memphis police burst into Tichenor's hotel room expecting an exchange of gunfire. Instead, Sergeant W.J. Raney walked calmly into the bedroom where Kelly was passed out with his wife, still inebriated from the previous night's gin binge. Raney thrust his shotgun into the pajama-clad belly of the intoxicated outlaw to announce that he was under arrest.

The red-eyed, heavy-lidded Kelly merely replied, "I've been waiting for ya."

Although the FBI ultimately received credit for Kelly's capture, providing the cue for Kelly's legendary plea: "Don't shoot, G-men!" the arrest was entirely the work of Memphis police department.

The FBI desperately wanted Machine Gun Kelly, whose publicity following the Urschel kidnapping suddenly made him a prime suspect in three bank-robbing homicides as well as one of the gunman in the Kansas City Massacre. While there was no hard evidence to connect Kelly to any of these crimes, the FBI used the occasion of Kelly's apprehension to bolster its own image. Director J. Edgar Hoover claimed to have coined the term "G (overnment)-men," possibly to ingratiate himself with Washington powers who still questioned the Bureau's overall efficiency in combating the country's crime crisis.

The major discrepancy in the Bureau's official record of Machine Gun Kelly's capture is that the arresting agents were said to have burst into the hotel room brandishing firearms. But FBI agents were not permitted to carry guns until May 1934. (Prior to this ruling, the FBI were definitely armed when Dillinger associate Eddie Green was gunned down on April 3, 1934, and, of course, during the raid on Little Bohemia just 19 days later.)

Despite the factual oversight, Hoover's public relations tool certainly did the trick. While a bewildered George Kelly sat in his jail cell awaiting extradition to Oklahoma, the phrase "G-man" was already being hyped throughout the country and was used as a warning call to all existing and upcoming public enemies.

Machine Gun Kelly and Kathryn received life sentences for their part in the Charles Urschel kidnapping. Kelly died in prison, while Kathryn was released and faded into obscurity.

Machine Gun Kelly, Kathryn Kelly and their various accomplices were all tried under the newly instated Lindbergh Federal Law.* When Kelly made his first entrance into the courtroom, he sported an egg-sized lump on his forehead and blood

---

*The Lindbergh Law was passed following the abduction and murder of the infant son of famed aviator Charles Lindbergh. The law defined kidnapping as a federal offense and punishable as such.

trickling from the corner of his mouth. As he and Kathryn were being escorted from their holding cells, Kathryn spotted her birth father and tried to go to him, only to be restrained by the prison guard. George tried to interfere and was pistol-whipped for his trouble by an overzealous guard.

The jury deliberated for less than two hours before deciding the fates of the defendants. For the first time, newsreel cameras were permitted inside a federal courtroom, and following the inevitable guilty verdict, Judge Edward S. Vaught's stern reading was recorded for posterity. All of the accused were given life sentences. Machine Gun Kelly was herded from the courtroom in manacles. He was imprisoned at Leavenworth, while Kathryn was transferred to a federal penitentiary in Cincinnati.

Even without Kathryn's encouragement, Kelly continued his tough-guy act with both the press and prison officials, promising that after he escaped from Leavenworth, he would break out his wife so that they could spend Christmas together. His threats were taken seriously enough that he was shipped to the island facility of Alcatraz, arriving there on September 4. Accompanying him were Albert Bates and Harvey Bailey. They would be among that penitentiary's first group of prisoners.

At first, Kelly tried to maintain his reputation by bragging to fellow inmates of his many crimes (most of which were embellished or sheer fiction). It didn't take long for the other convicts to see through his incessant boasting to the point of avoiding him, and Kelly was soon relegated to his true status as AZ-117.

His years in Alcatraz were uneventful. He worked in the prison laundry, held an administrative job in the industry offices and even found spiritual redemption by serving as an altar boy in the prison chapel. He apparently experienced remorse at his past life and wrote frequent letters to Charles Urschel asking for his forgiveness. These letters all went unacknowledged. In one of his notes, Kelly said, "...these five words seen written on the walls of my cell: 'Nothing can be worth this.' " Eventually, Warden J.J. Johnston began referring to the once-notorious gangster as a model prisoner.

Machine Gun Kelly was transferred to Leavenworth in 1951, where he died of a heart attack on July 18, 1954, the day of his 59th birthday.

Kathryn was released from the Cincinnati Workhouse in June 1958 together with her mother. She worked as a book-keeper in an Oklahoma hospital before drifting into anonymity.

Although the name Machine Gun Kelly is still remembered today, much of the truth surrounding his criminal exploits has caused many to question his placement among the pantheon of great American outlaws. The FBI account of his capture afforded him some notoriety and was dramatized on screen in *The FBI Story* starring Jimmy Stewart. But sadly, the reputation he tried so hard to live up to became a mockery as the once-feared gunman became more frequently known as "Pop Gun Kelly."

CHAPTER ELEVEN

The Kansas City Massacre

"My God, it's just like Chicago!"
–A witness to the event

AT APPROXIMATELY 7:20 AM on Saturday, June 17, 1933, Union Station in Kansas City, Missouri, was its usual hustle and bustle of activity, serving the transportation needs of middle America. The cacophony of sounds emanating from within its vast structure was occasionally punctuated by loudspeaker announcements of arrivals and departures. The people milling about the station were a cross-section of types, ranging from businessmen and merchants to casual travelers. Families and friends both welcomed back and said emotional goodbyes to loved ones as personal everyday mini-dramas were played out inside its cavernous confines. Outdoors, the temperature was a comfortable 71°F. It looked to be a pleasant day.

Seconds later, the morning exploded into violence as machine-gun fire suddenly erupted in the plaza parking lot. People inside the terminal had no idea what was happening until screaming citizens began rushing inside.

"They're killing everybody!" one woman shouted frantically.

By the time the gunfire ceased, five men were dead and two others wounded. Bloodied bodies lay twisted inside the bullet-riddled shell of a 1932 Chevrolet and sprawled on the pavement next to the vehicle.

What no one immediately knew was that six of the victims were law enforcement officers, three of whom were agents with the U.S. Bureau of Investigation. The seventh man, dead with most of his skull blown away and a pathetic red wig askew against what was left of his bald head, was the criminal the lawmen were preparing to return to Leavenworth, from whence he had engineered another of his famous escapes. His name was Frank Nash.

Nicknamed "Jelly" because of his uncanny ability to slip into banks and out of imprisonment, Nash was one of the most successful bank robbers of the period, with ties to the Barker-Karpis Gang, the Machine Gun Kelly Mob and most of the other big-name bandit outfits.

The USBI had been chasing the slippery bandit for three years ever since he'd again proven the validity of his moniker by walking out of Leavenworth. More specifically, he'd escaped the home of Warden Thomas White, where the personable convict had been granted trusty privileges and allowed to cook meals for the warden and his family.

Frank Nash never achieved the notoriety of other bank robbers of his day, but he enjoyed a career just as colorful. He was born in Indiana in 1887. His father, John O. Nash, moved the family to Oklahoma, where he established a prosperous hotel in Hobart in 1902. When Frank came of age, he went to work in the kitchen as a cook. His father eventually turned over the ownership of the hotel to his daughter Alice and her husband, John Long. While Frank displayed a definite

Frank "Jelly" Nash, the central figure in the Kansas City Massacre, who likely died without ever knowing the true role he was playing

flair for preparing meals, he quickly grew tired of kitchen work. He found clerking at the front desk even less stimulating.

Frank's craving for adventure finally found fulfillment when he turned to small-time burglary in and around the Hobart area. While the scores were penny-ante, they provided his dreary life with excitement. By 1913, Frank had teamed with two accomplices, "Humpie" Wartman and John Huber, and the trio enjoyed a successful run of residential and commercial burglaries. But their luck turned sour when they suspected that "Humpie" had talked to the police.

"Can't believe you'd do this to us, Hump," Nash sighed, sounding as hurt as a betrayed father.

Hump was coaxed into admitting his duplicity with several potent shots of whiskey. Nash then calmly pulled out his pistol and shot him dead.

"Sorry, Hump," he said with genuine regret.

Nash and Huber were soon arrested for the crime. While awaiting trial for murder, their one consolation was that the hotel catered all of their meals, compliments of Frank's sister Alice.

The first trial, held in July, resulted in a hung jury. The second trial brought in a guilty verdict, and on September 13, Nash was sent to the state penitentiary at McAlester where the court ruled he would serve out a life sentence.

He was registered as Prisoner #4458 and forced to take his place among the nameless nonentities exposed to the cold confines of penitentiary life. What Nash found hardest to endure was the utter lack of cultural pleasures at McAlester. For a man of Nash's refined appetites, this made for a particularly difficult transition. Besides being denied fine dining privileges, like those he had been afforded at Hobart, he also could not indulge his love for classical literature, particularly Shakespeare.

Nash worked at becoming a model prisoner so that he might soon be made a trusty. His rehabilitation seemed so complete that after serving only five years, he was granted a full pardon when he expressed his desire to serve his country overseas during World War I. Nash's patriotic gesture took him no further than the nearest hotel in Hobart, where he stayed secluded while he plotted his next criminal endeavor.

Sheriff's deputies arrested Nash on October 18, 1919, after a series of minor robberies made him the prime suspect in a bank job pulled in Cordell, Oklahoma. This time the charge was dropped. Undeterred, Nash pulled together a new crew to hit the bank in the Oklahoma farming community of Corn. Nash wasn't as lucky this time. He was apprehended, convicted of burglary using explosives and sent back to McAlester on August 4, 1920, to begin a 25-year stretch.

Nash's recapture was not all bad news. It resulted in a friendship with Al Spencer, who was a true crossover from the era of frontier outlaw to contemporary gangster. Oklahoma-born, he was five years older than Nash and entertained the younger man with tales of graduating from cattle rustler and horse thief to full-fledged bank robber. He boasted that he was given the title "King of the Osage," referring to his preferred stomping grounds in the Osage Hills.

Nash learned a lot from Spencer, but the older thief wasn't planning to stick around long enough to complete Nash's education. He escaped from the penitentiary on January 27, 1922. He'd invited Nash to come along, but Nash declined, not willing to risk a bullet in so daring a maneuver.

Nash was an interesting contradiction. Despite his apparent boldness in burglaries or bank heists, he possessed a genuine fear of being killed in a jailbreak. His fear proved ultimately prophetic.

Nash once again effected his own quiet prison break when he applied for and was granted a temporary leave, which he claimed was for business reasons. In December, he walked from the gates of McAlester and quickly joined Al Spencer and the team Spencer had carefully assembled during his 11 months of freedom. Many of the men were rough-hewn independents who agreed to team up only on a limited partnership. But when they joined forces, they were formidable.

Under Spencer's leadership, they rode like true Western desperadoes. They robbed boomtown banks and post offices armed not with Thompson submachine guns, but rather sawed-off shotguns. They hit with a savvy and frequency that would have made the James boys proud. Some say that in a 20-month period, the Spencer Gang robbed as many as 22 banks. Others swear they easily knocked over twice that number. But many doubters claimed that the legend simply grew out of proportion, and that many of the heists attributed to the Spencer Gang were committed by other maverick bands.

One score for which Spencer and his crew deserved full credit was when they pulled off what may have been the country's last great horseback train robbery on Tuesday, August 21, 1923. They held up the train just outside of Spencer's old Osage County stomping grounds. Spencer, Nash and three others galloped off with $20,000 in bonds and cash from the Katy Limited passenger train. The heist went off smoothly except for one incident. Nash's temper flared during the early moments of the robbery, when he became anxious and pistol-whipped train fireman Byron Tower, leaving him with a serious concussion. Still, they rode off, although not exactly into the sunset.

Al Spencer had barely a month left to live to enjoy the rewards of his labor. On September 20, lawmen responding to a tip located the criminal in hiding just south of the Kansas border. A posse set up an ambush deep in the brush bordering the dirt trail where he had often been seen walking.

Sure enough, near sunset, a figure curiously armed with a rifle and automatic pistol ambled from the woods. The lawmen quickly flashed on their car headlights, capturing the suspect in their glare. They issued the half-hearted command for him to halt and identify himself. Instead, the outlaw panicked and bolted towards the road.

The posse opened fire, and Al Spencer dropped with at least three slugs in his body. Reportedly, they discovered thousands of dollars in bonds on his corpse.

"Reckon we got the right man," one of the posse remarked.

Not long after Spencer's killing, the other Osage train robbers, with the exception of Frank Nash, were rounded up and brought to justice.

"Jelly" Nash remained on the run until late autumn 1923, when he was discovered working as a ranch hand in Mexico. His boss refused to turn him over to U.S. authorities while Nash was still employed in the country and so compromised by sending him over the border on a bogus errand. Officials quickly arrested him.

On March 3, 1924, Nash was sentenced to 25 years at Leavenworth for robbery and assault, where he was assigned prison number 20769. And then, on Memorial Day, May 30, 1933, three years after he walked away from the kitchen of Leavenworth warden Thomas White, he helped mastermind the escape of 11 convicts from the Kansas state prison at Lansing.

These were a dangerous lot, consisting primarily of murderers and bank robbers. Prominent among the group were Harvey Bailey and Wilbur Underhill. Known as the "Tri-State Terror," Underhill was serving a life term for murdering a Wichita policeman. He was such an incorrigible prisoner that three of his four years served were spent in solitary confinement. Bailey was another crook serving hard time. He was a brilliant bank robber and tactician, whose path would cross with most of the successful bandit outfits of the time, including the Barker-Karpis outfit. "Old Harve," so called because of his prematurely graying hair, had so assimilated himself into the fabric of the underworld and had achieved such notoriety that he was even briefly considered as one of the gunmen in the St. Valentine's Day Massacre.

Since his escape from Leavenworth, Nash had already been instrumental in the escape of bank robbers Thomas Holden and Francis Keating (future associates of Machine Gun Kelly). On July 8, 1932, while Nash was enjoying a game of golf with the pair and Harvey Bailey at the Old

Mission Country Club, local detectives closed in on the criminals. Holden, Keating and Bailey were taken into custody. Nash, who was luckily playing out another hole, witnessed the arrest of the others and silently slipped into the nearby bushes. He then apparently teamed up with the Barker-Karpis Gang, participating in several holdups before taking part in the Lansing escape.

Nash underwent plastic surgery to straighten his crooked nose, and also purchased a toupee to cover his trademark bald head. These modifications were hardly effective given that Nash's unique bird-like appearance was plastered on wanted posters throughout the country. But disguise wasn't nearly as important as the protective umbrella both he and his new bride, a divorcee named Frances Luce, were afforded by the underworld in Hot Springs, Arkansas.

Nash remained a wanted man, with federal agents and local police searching for him in five states. Finally, through the cooperation of an embittered Holden and Keating, federal officials learned of Nash's whereabouts and moved in to arrest him. On the morning of Friday, June 16, agents Frank C. Smith and F. Joseph Lackey from the Bureau of Investigation's Oklahoma City office, together with McAlester Police Chief Otto Reed, apprehended Nash while the fugitive sat drinking a bottle of beer inside the White Front Cigar Store.

Nash surrendered immediately. As he was escorted from the premises, the store's owner, Richard Galatas, a man with heavy ties to the city's underworld, placed calls to several of Nash's associates.

Hot Springs was a town drowning in corruption, and even Agent Smith later said, "It was a wonder we weren't killed when we took Nash."

The agents drove into Fort Smith. At 8:30 PM, they herded their manacled prisoner aboard the Missouri Pacific Flyer headed for Kansas City, where they were to be met the following morning by federal agents and local police officers, who would accompany them on the final leg of their trip to the Big House at Leavenworth.

Realizing that Nash's underworld friends might want to repay a favor by releasing him from custody, the agents kept their route a secret. As the train sped through the clear starlit night towards its destination, the agents tried to ease the tension by engaging in light banter with Nash, teasing him about his ill-fitting red wig.

"Cost me a hundred bucks," Nash said with a casual shrug. "You do what you can."

But when one of the agents leaned forward and tried to tug off what he perceived was a phony mustache, Nash quickly recoiled.

"That's the real thing!" he exclaimed.

Arrangements had been made through J. Edgar Hoover to have Special Agents Reed E. Vetterli, who was in charge of the Kansas City office, and 31-year-old Raymond J. Caffrey waiting at Union Station. Two trusted Kansas City plainclothes police officers, W.J. Grooms and Frank Hermanson, were also recruited to assist with the transfer.

Lackey instructed Nash and Reed to stay put inside the stateroom while he went to the loading platform to find his contacts. Establishing their credentials to be legitimate, Lackey then asked the men to help him survey the immediate area. All were satisfied that nothing appeared out of the ordinary.

"Don't lower your guard, men," Lackey cautioned. "Not until we see that metal gate slam shut on Nash."

Lackey went back to the train to retrieve Nash. The four federal agents and three policemen formed a circle around the bandit as they walked through the terminal towards the outdoor plaza where the transporting car was parked. Each of the lawmen was armed. Reed and Lackey carried shotguns; the others were equipped with pistols.

As they exited the station, they walked briskly to Agent Caffrey's 1932 Chevy sedan, which was parked directly in front of the east entrance of Union Station. Caffrey unlocked the door and eased a handcuffed Nash into the backseat. Agent Lackey suddenly halted the procedure, deciding that he wanted Nash to sit up front. As Nash was maneuvered into the front seat through the driver's side, Lackey, Smith and Reed started to slide into the backseat. Caffrey was preparing to take his place behind the wheel.

A vigilant Lackey suddenly noticed two men emerge from behind a nearby parked car. Both men were armed with machine guns.

Before Lackey could utter a warning to his colleagues, one of the gunmen, later described as "heavyset," shouted: "Put 'em up! Up! Up!"

The lawmen froze as another machine-gun-toting hood suddenly materialized next to a green Plymouth parked only six feet from the Chevy. What followed has long been a point of conjecture given the conflicting accounts by witnesses. Some claim that Officer Grooms impulsively pulled his pistol and fired two shots, winging the heavyset gunman in the arm.

Others say that no such provocation occurred, and that the gunmen opened fire when the heavyset man gave the booming command: "Let 'em have it!"

In any event, sudden bursts of machine-gun fire raked across the Chevy, taking down the unprepared lawmen. Bystanders ran screaming for cover as bullets whizzed through the air. Many people ducked behind cars and other solid structures, while some merely dropped flat to the pavement. Parents grabbed their children and tried to hustle them away from the violence.

Witness reports later confirmed that policemen Grooms and Hermanson were the first casualties. Wounded when the gunfire commenced, both officers, along with Agent Vetterli, who was hit in the arm, dropped flat to the ground. Vetterli rolled out of range of the machine-gun spray that was now leveled at the two prone lawmen. Officers Grooms and Hermanson died instantly.

Ironically, it was Frank Nash who, either by accident or design, was the next victim of the carnage. Witnesses remember hearing him scream: "For God's sake, don't kill me!" Then the bandit, who'd always had a fear of being killed by police bullets, had half his head blown away, not by the law, but by his apparent rescuers.

Agent Caffrey was shot through the head in the initial burst of machine-gun fire. The lawyer-turned-G-man from Nebraska died en route to the hospital. Oklahoma Police Chief Otto Reed, who had assisted the federal men in their arrest of Nash and had come along only to see Frank Nash in government custody, was killed when machine-gun bullets blasted into his chest. Agents Smith and Lackey fell forward in the rear seat of the Chevrolet once the shooting began. Lackey was hit three times in the spine, but survived. Agent Smith was the only man to escape the massacre unharmed.

No more than 30 seconds after it began, the assault was over. The gunmen brazenly raced towards the bullet-shattered car to examine their marksmanship.

"They're all dead!" one of them shouted. "Okay, let's get the hell outta here."

The three murderers turned and ran towards a dark-colored Chevy. A brave Kansas City policeman rushed from Union Station and fired several shots with his service revolver at the fleeing gunmen, all of whom hopped into their vehicle and sped out of the plaza, driving in a westerly direction. For several moments, complete stillness settled over Union Station. Then people began to converge on the bloody scene, horror-struck at what they had just observed. Curiosity-seekers also began to

The aftermath of the Kansas City Massacre, one of the bloodiest events in the annals of American crime

descend, checking out the bodies with wide-eyed gazes and looking for opportunities to scoop up grisly souvenirs.

More than 70 years later, the question remains unanswered: What was the true intent behind the Kansas City Massacre?

Theories abound.

Because Kansas City, Missouri, was a hotbed for criminal activity, and Frank Nash knew more than most about its corrupt policies, many have claimed that the Union Station slaughter was not a bungled attempt to free Nash but rather a way to silence him.

Intense investigation led federal authorities to pinpoint the masterminds behind the Kansas City Massacre as Richard Galatas, Herbert Farmer, Louis Stacci and Frank Mulloy, who were known outlaw friends of Frank Nash. On October 24, 1934, the four men were indicted by a Federal Grand Jury and found guilty of "conspiracy to cause the escape of a federal prisoner from the custody of the United States." Each was sentenced to a two-year term in prison and ordered to pay a $10,000 fine.

But the identities of the Union Station gunmen remain a mystery to this day. Within days of the shooting, likely candidates included Charles Arthur "Pretty Boy" Floyd, his partner at the time, Adam "Eddie" Richetti and two others who had more than a passing acquaintance with Nash as well as significant ties to the Kansas City underworld—Verne Miller and Wilbur Underhill, "the Tri-State Terror."

Although the FBI could never substantiate its case, the Bureau always maintained that Floyd and Richetti were the principle gunmen, and that it was Pretty Boy (the "heavyset one") who gave the order to open fire. The eyewitness accounts that "positively" identified Floyd at the scene were tentative at best.

Numerous facts support Floyd's claim of innocence. Floyd and Richetti were on the run at the time, and at Floyd's suggestion, the two had come to Kansas City because it was a safe haven when the heat was on. Floyd had had enough experience in K.C. to know that as long as he stayed out of trouble and dropped a few dollars into the right pockets, he'd be well taken care of. It seems unlikely and inconceivable that a man tagged as one of the country's leading public enemies would even be tempted to jeopardize his privilege by agreeing to partake in a daylight criminal act where his famous face, plastered on posters and popular magazine covers, would be instantly recognized by hundreds of potential witnesses.

Yet Floyd's presence in the city at the time had value because it provided the Kansas City underworld with a convenient fall guy. Apparently, what these organized gangsters were seeking was a maverick outlaw and well-publicized killer who could be easily identified and thus assume the heat for their own criminal machinations. Who better than Pretty Boy Floyd, habitué of Kansas City, and at the time, the country's most notorious criminal?

The rest was all cosmetics. It wasn't difficult to find a gunman of the correct physical dimensions to stand in for Pretty Boy. Although it was mid-June, they further camouflaged their Floyd double by clothing him a heavy overcoat and low-brimmed fedora.

Professor Kent Ladd Steckmesser, who spent a great deal of time researching the facts of the case, reported his findings in a 1970 magazine article, reiterating that Floyd's only crime was his presence in Kansas City. Steckmesser goes on to say, "The job is too much at variance with the usual Floyd pattern." He concluded, "The actual machine gunners were killed by the mob for having botched their assignment."

It is here that Verne Miller fits into the intrigue. He may be the only one of whom it can be said with any degree of certainty played a role in the massacre. Miller was an expert marksman, proving his mettle as a machine-gunner during World War I. Upon his discharge, he returned to his home state of South Dakota where his prowess with firearms landed him a job as a policeman in Huron. Later, he was elected to Sheriff, a position to which he was re-nominated. But Miller felt restricted operating within the confines of the law and believed his skills could be more profitably utilized working the other side of the fence, so he became a criminal. After a series of arrests, he moved to St. Paul, Minnesota, and later Chicago, where he was quickly employed as a Syndicate gunman. During a brief stay in New York, he reportedly worked

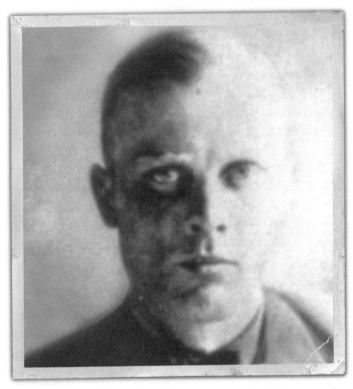

Vernon C. Miller remains the most intriguing factor in the
Kansas City Massacre. His underworld affiliations present
him not only as a key participant, but likely recruiter of the
other gunmen employed in the Union Station killings.
Reputedly, his background as a lawman also includes a brief
association with Al Capone and the Chicago Mob, whose
feathers the arrogantly independent Miller also apparently
ruffled. Miller's own violent death, in which his corpse was
trussed up like a turkey, his flesh pierced by ice picks and
seared with a flatiron before his skull was crushed by a blunt
object, bore the hallmarks of a planned execution, perhaps
even a vendetta, leading the FBI to remark: "He turned the
heat on the whole underworld."

as a "Murder Incorporated" assassin under Louis Lepke, one of the new breed of gangsters who, along with Lucky Luciano and Bugsy Siegel, was responsible for forming a national crime syndicate.

Following the Kansas City Massacre, Miller and his current girlfriend, Vivian Mathias, traveled to Chicago. On October 31, 1933, federal agents raided Mathias' apartment. Miller escaped, but agents took Mathias into custody and charged her with harboring a fugitive.

Almost a month later, on November 29, the mutilated corpse of Verne Miller was discovered in a ditch outside Detroit, Michigan. He was obviously the victim of a Syndicate hit and was beaten and tortured before he was killed.

"Someone got the drop on him," a criminal confidant said later. "Miller was too smart not to smell a trap."

The question of whether Miller's brutal murder was connected to his participation in the Kansas City Massacre has never been resolved. Some claim that the hotheaded Miller was killed because of an altercation he'd had with an associate of "Longy" Zwillman, then head of the New Jersey underworld.

Soon Floyd and Richetti would also be removed from the picture by federal intervention. Floyd swore with his dying breath that he'd played no part in the massacre, and Richetti walked into the gas chamber maintaining his silence.

Another possible suspect, Wilbur Underhill, likewise died without saying much. He was celebrating his honeymoon with his new bride in Shawnee, Oklahoma, when federal agents surrounded their cottage on New Year's Day, 1934, and ordered Underhill to surrender. The "Tri-State Terror" pulled out two pistols and began firing, dashing from window to window. The agents responded by blasting more than 1000 bullets into the cottage. Underhill, hit at least a dozen times, finally ran from the cottage clad only in his underclothes. He fired shotgun blasts at his pursuers and managed to stumble his way into town, where he broke through the front window of a furniture store and collapsed. He was taken to the hospital in McAlester, where he died five days later on January 6.

His final words were simply, "Tell the boys I'm coming home."

Gangster James "Blackie" Audette stated conclusively in 1954 writings that the actual "hitters" were Verne Miller and two lesser-league gunmen—brothers Maurice and Homer Denning—and possibly a fourth party named William "Solly" Weissman.

"I knowed (it was them) because I seen with my own eyes who was in that car," wrote Audette.

To further support Audette's argument that the Syndicate had ordered the hit, Weissman's corpse soon turned up in the same mangled condition as Miller's, while Maurice and Homer Denning's bodies were never found at all. Audette said that the gunmen were killed simply because they were hired to do a job and knew the identities of the men who had ordered it.

He also balked at the claim that Nash's murder wasn't deliberate. According to Audette, his "liberators" could not have failed to recognize Nash (even with his red wig), seated in the front seat of the car wildly waving his handcuffed hands. Audette maintained that from the moment of his capture in Hot Springs, Frank Nash was a dead man.

Why was Nash targeted for assassination? The most likely reason is that his breed of criminal had become archaic by modern standards, one whose mere presence posed a threat to the changes occurring within the nation's underworld. Just as the criminal environment was undergoing transition in other major centers such as Chicago, New York and Detroit, Kansas City was also growing with the times. Outlaws like Frank Nash and Pretty Boy Floyd could no longer be tolerated because their maverick escapades attracted too much attention, making them liabilities to the new order.

The Kansas City Massacre remains one of the darkest days in the history of 20th-century America. But because of the magnitude of its violence and blatant disregard of justice officers, the incident ultimately precipitated changes in the government's stand against crime.

Previously, J. Edgar Hoover's agents were merely investigators who, while often exposed to dangerous situations, were denied firearm protection and given minimal jurisdiction. After the slaughter at Union Station, Hoover took advantage of public outrage to demand that his office be given the right to take a more active stand against the ruthless violence perpetrated by the country's growing criminal element.

With the support of U.S. Attorney Homer Cummings, legislative measures went before Congress, and on May 18, 1934, President Franklin Roosevelt passed into law several statutes that would increase the Bureau's jurisdiction and broaden its authority. As part of its new image, the former Bureau of Investigation was renamed the Federal Bureau of Investigation on July 1, 1935. Agents were permitted to carry firearms and given almost a free hand in their pursuit and apprehension of criminals.

Equipped with better-trained field personnel and advanced procedural methods of investigation, the FBI and local law enforcement agencies marshaled their resources to complete the cleanup of the few renegade outlaws who still roamed the Midwest. But these were a motley bunch lacking the cunning and pure survival instincts of their predecessors. As such, they remained a minor menace, and their notoriety and ultimate fates were mere historical footnotes compared to the lasting legacies of the Dustbowl Desperadoes.

Notes on Sources

Aurandt, Paul. *More of Paul Harvey's The Rest of the Story*. New York: William Morrow, 1980.

Bruns, Roger A. *The Bandit Kings*. New York: Crown Publishers, 1995.

Clarens, Carlos. *Crime Movies*. New York: W.W. Norton, 1980.

Girardin, G. Russell and William J. Helmer. *Dillinger: The Untold Story*. Bloomington and Indianapolis: Indiana University Press, 1994.

Karpis, Alvin and Bill Trent. *The Alvin Karpis Story*. New York: Berkley, 1971.

Karpis, Alvin and Robert Livesey. *On the Rock*. Don Mills: Musson, 1980.

Kurland, Michael. *A Gallery of Rogues*. New York: Prentice Hall, 1994.

Louderback, Lew. *The Bad Ones: Gangsters of the '30s and Their Molls*. New York: Fawcett, 1968.

Nash, Jay Robert. *Bloodletters and Badmen: A Narrative Encyclopedia of American Criminals from the Pilgrims to the Present.* New York: M. Evans, 1973.

Nash, Jay Robert and Ron Offen. *Dillinger: Dead or Alive?* Chicago: Henry Regnery, 1970.

Steinbeck, John. *The Grapes of Wrath.* New York: Viking Press, 1939.

Toland, John. *The Dillinger Days.* New York: Random House, 1963.

Treherne, John. *The Strange History of Bonnie and Clyde.* London: Jonathan Cape, 1984.

Wallis, Michael. *Pretty Boy.* New York: St. Martin's Press, 1992.

Whitehead, Don. *The FBI Story: A Report to the People.* New York: Random House, 1956.

STONE WALLACE

Stone Wallace is an accomplished author, as well as an actor, director, celebrity interviewer and broadcaster. In his role as a journalist, he has had the privilege to interview celebrities such as John Agar, Dolores Fuller, Coleen Gray, Lloyd Nolan, Robert Stack and Herbert L. Strock. He has published five novels, including the bestseller *Blood Moon*. *Dustbowl Desperadoes: Gangsters of the Dirty '30s* is his second work of non-fiction and his first book for Folklore Publishing.

Among his acting credits, Stone can count appearances on both stage and screen in a variety of roles for theater, television and film. He has also lent his talents to the airwaves for several radio projects, and he has taken a turn behind the scenes directing a production of *The Diary of Anne Frank*.